I AM

VENERABLE CONCEPCIÓN CABRERA DE ARMIDA (CONCHITA)

I Am
Eucharistic Meditations on the Gospel

ALBA·HOUSE   NEW·YORK

SOCIETY OF ST. PAUL, 2187 VICTORY BLVD., STATEN ISLAND, NEW YORK 10314

ST PAULS

Library of Congress Cataloging-in-Publication Data

Conchita, 1862-1937.
   I Am : Eucharistic meditations on the Gospel / Concepción Cabrera de Armida.
      p. cm.
      ISBN:0-8189-0890-4
      1. Lord's Supper—Meditations. 2. Bible N.T. Gospels—Meditations. 3. Catholic
   Church—Prayer-books and devotions—English.   I. Title.

   BX2169.C66 2001
   242—dc21

                                                                00-069965

Produced and designed in the United States of America by the
Fathers and Brothers of the Society of St. Paul,
2187 Victory Boulevard, Staten Island, New York 10314-6603,
as part of their communications apostolate.

ISBN:0-8189-0890-4

Printing Information:

Current Printing - first digit   1   2   3   4   5   6   7   8   9   10

Year of Current Printing - first year shown

2001   2002   2003   2004   2005   2006   2007   2008   2009   2010

Table of Contents

Foreword

God, our Father, creator of the Universe wants to come close to us human beings in the Person of His Son made man. "This presence of Jesus Christ makes possible our encounter with Him, as the Son sent by the Father, as the Lord of life Who communicates His Spirit to us" (cf. *Ecclesia in America*, 7).

Jesus continues to be present among us in the EUCHARIST, a real and mysterious presence that transforms us in His image and likeness. This presence speaks to us, favors us, gifts us and strengthens us for the difficult journey through life.

Some Christians experience this presence more, listen to the voice of Jesus, engrave in their wills His attitudes. This is what a sister of ours, CONCEPCIÓN CABRERA DE ARMIDA, Mexican wife and mother did. She relates to us her inflamed dialogues with the Eucharistic Jesus, the desires of her docile heart to the wishes of the Divine Heart.

This message continues to live on and invites us into the joyful and radiant existence of the disciples of Jesus.

I am sure that our *faith* in Jesus will be strengthened by reading these dialogues of Conchita with her Lord. It will increase our *hope* in Him as Savior of the world. Our heart will be inflamed, fulfilling *His will that we love* one another as brothers and sisters.

Let us celebrate the Jubilee of the Incarnation of Jesus in the womb of Mary, who has paid her maternal visit to our country at the hill of Tepeyac!

Given at the Archbishop's Office in Mexico, 15th of August of the year one thousand nine hundred ninety-nine.

✠ Cardinal Rivera Carrera
Archbishop of Mexico

Biblical Abbreviations

OLD TESTAMENT

Genesis	Gn	Nehemiah	Ne	Baruch	Ba
Exodus	Ex	Tobit	Tb	Ezekiel	Ezk
Leviticus	Lv	Judith	Jdt	Daniel	Dn
Numbers	Nb	Esther	Est	Hosea	Ho
Deuteronomy	Dt	1 Maccabees	1 M	Joel	Jl
Joshua	Jos	2 Maccabees	2 M	Amos	Am
Judges	Jg	Job	Jb	Obadiah	Ob
Ruth	Rt	Psalms	Ps	Jonah	Jon
1 Samuel	1 S	Proverbs	Pr	Micah	Mi
2 Samuel	2 S	Ecclesiastes	Ec	Nahum	Na
1 Kings	1 K	Song of Songs	Sg	Habakkuk	Hab
2 Kings	2 K	Wisdom	Ws	Zephaniah	Zp
1 Chronicles	1 Ch	Sirach	Si	Haggai	Hg
2 Chronicles	2 Ch	Isaiah	Is	Malachi	Ml
Ezra	Ezr	Jeremiah	Jr	Zechariah	Zc
		Lamentations	Lm		

NEW TESTAMENT

Matthew	Mt	Ephesians	Eph	Hebrews	Heb
Mark	Mk	Philippians	Ph	James	Jm
Luke	Lk	Colossians	Col	1 Peter	1 P
John	Jn	1 Thessalonians	1 Th	2 Peter	2 P
Acts	Ac	2 Thessalonians	2 Th	1 John	1 Jn
Romans	Rm	1 Timothy	1 Tm	2 John	2 Jn
1 Corinthians	1 Cor	2 Timothy	2 Tm	3 John	3 Jn
2 Corinthians	2 Cor	Titus	Tt	Jude	Jude
Galatians	Gal	Philemon	Phm	Revelation	Rv

Introduction

It always moves me to hear the words of our Savior, when He said:

"Philip, after I have been with you all this time, you still do not know Me?"[1]

It seems to me that this heartfelt complaint of Jesus is coming from tabernacles everywhere. All this time and still you do not know Me!

Furthermore, why don't we know Him? Because we do not think about Him or love Him enough.

But, is it possible for us to know Him on our own? O, no! That is why Jesus Himself, with the power and fire that all the words in His Holy Gospel contain, says to us

"I AM…."

These meditations, whose insights are given to us by Jesus, will help us appreciate more the Sacrament of the Eucharist.

Holy Spirit, enlighten our minds to know Jesus and inflame our hearts with holy love.

Virgin Mary, you who knew Jesus so intimately, bless us, enkindle our souls with love for your Divine Son and teach us to live His virtues.

---

[1] Jn 14:9.

1

I Am...
(Ex 3:14)

> The God of majesty, thrice holy,
> comes to the nothingness of His
> creatures to raise them up, making
> them holy, enveloping them in His
> mercy and love.

"I am Who am," and nobody can understand all the meaning within these sublime, divine words that could only be pronounced by God Himself.

And this definition of the thrice holy God was heard from the burning bush by Moses, barefooted, stepping on thorns, because only in pain can the confidences of God be heard.

"I am Who am," that is, I am the One Who is eternally infinite, the One Who has no beginning, the One Who will have no end; the Almighty, Immense, Uncreated, God of love, Who is holy by essence, the Creator of all that exists or can exist, the wholly Unique One, the Sovereign Who created everything for Himself, the God of Kindness, Who *possesses* Himself and *gives* Himself without measure; *He Who is!* More cannot be said.

From this infinite Being in three Persons I proceed, the Divine Word made flesh, the second Person of the Blessed Trinity, equal to the Father and the Holy Spirit in Power, Wisdom, Kindness and every other attribute. I come to embrace fallen humanity, taking on your nature to bring you up to heaven.

Only a God could satisfy the offense to God, and love, love alone made Me offer Myself to the Father for your good and descend into the womb of a virgin, the straw of a manger, the sweat of a carpenter shop, the affronts, the sufferings and the humiliations of Calvary, to death on the Cross and to be a perpetual Victim on the altar for as long as there would be someone to feed on My Body, My Blood and My Life itself.

God touched you, enveloped you but you could not come close to Him! That is why I came to make Myself Eucharist, to live at your side, hiding My splendor, descending into your heart to enrich and transform it. Creation, Redemption and Communion are proofs that I am Love, that I have always been and will never cease to be Love.

Come then to your Savior, to your Jesus, Who has made Himself bread to feed you. Come to the God of your hopes. Come, and like Moses, adore your God and Lord.

Act of Thanksgiving

God of Love, You did not wish to be happy without man, and without needing anyone, sought the love of Your creatures. Thank You because You wanted to need me to communicate Your love to me and to manifest it to my brothers.

He is everything, I am nothing. He is eternal in His perfections, I am limited. He is merciful, I am in misery. He humbled Himself for my love; I am proud, hard, insensitive to so much tenderness.

You said one day, *"My Father is always working and I am working too."*[2] Therefore Jesus, cleanse me, purify and transform

---

[2]   Jn 5:17.

my *non-being* into something virtuous, vivifying me with Your contact.

O Mary, Daughter, Spouse, and Mother of Him Who *is* by and of *Himself*, from Whom *everything is!*, obtain for me the grace of being the living image of Jesus on earth, loving, consoling, suffering and denying myself for others. Amen.

Thoughts and Life

Whoever does not have love, does not have life and the degree of perfection that we have before God is in direct proportion to the degree of our love.

Commitment

Jesus, I will prove the sincerity of my affection, conquering myself today *in what costs me most*. When one wants, one can. What a great truth!

+ Lord, I will offer You many acts of love in favor of priests and families.

2

I Am the Beginning of All Things
(Cf. Jn 1:3-4; Jn 8:24)

> God, cause of the flourishing of all life, comes to His creatures who are dust and ashes to communicate to them the Divine Seed that never dies.

"All things came to be through the Word of the Father and without Him nothing came to be."[3]

"Well, who are You?" The Jews asked Me one day: *"I am the source of all that is."*[4] *"And if they do not believe that I am, they will die in their sins."*[5]

This is certain: I am the source of all things in heaven and on earth, on the sea and in the abyss, the stars and the trees, the flowers, the fruits and all that is created and will be created!

I am the principle of all life, of nature and of grace. Everything has its beginning in Me. *"All things were created through Me and for Me"*[6]: the light, movement, intelligence, all being and life takes life and being from Me. I am the One Who vivifies all things and without Me all would fall back into non-being.

---

[3] Jn 1:3-4.
[4] Cf. Jn 1:1.
[5] Jn 8:24.
[6] Cf. Col 1:16.

"In the beginning, I already was."[7] I loved you and you occupied My mind. For you there is past and future but for Me all is present. My glance envelops all in a single point in time that contains all eternity. At that point I rescued you because I loved you. I offered Myself to the Father for you in sacrifice.

In truth I say to you: *"Before Abraham came to be, I am."*[8] I myself am immutable eternity and all my perfections and attributes are enclosed in it. If I were not eternal and without beginning and *the beginning of all things*, I would not be God. But I am!

I am God Who became man out of love, *Who wanted to suffer and be an expiatory victim for sin*, honoring God, My Father, giving Him infinite glory.

Know Me Who is your beginning. Live by faith, honoring Me with your works and know that I took a human body of Mary and made Myself bread in the Eucharist, attracted by the image of the Trinity that I put in you solely for the joy of making you happy.

Be not afraid. Come, "I take delight in the children of men, playing on the surface of the earth."[9]

Act of Thanksgiving

My God, I adore Your greatness, I know Your tenderness. Your majesty humbles me, Your love calls me, attracts me, inspires my confidence. You are the God of Mt. Sinai, also of the manger, Calvary and the Eucharist.

Your power dazzles me, but I am drawn to You by Your mercy. *"In the beginning You were and in You was the life,"*[10] but

---

[7] Cf. Jn 1:1.
[8] Jn 8:58.
[9] Pr 8:31.
[10] Jn 1:1, 4.

You were mine and You were for me. In You there is no past, nor future, that is why You have always had me present in Your Heart.

I know that "You came to Your own and they did not receive You,"[11] but I do receive You with all my love.

Leave in heaven all Your greatness and splendor. I will see them some day, hoping in Your mercy. For now come within my reach as Bread from heaven. Come as little as You were sleeping in the arms of Mary, or as You were at work in Nazareth, because thus You seem to me closer than when You fashioned the world. Come, Jesus. Filled with gratitude for You, I adore You.

Mary, make me love your Son Jesus as the Principle behind all things, not with a fear that paralyzes and discourages, but with a love that knows no limits.

Thoughts and Life

Everything that happens will be precious to me, seeing in them the will of God from whence everything proceeds, from that Beginning without beginning.

Commitment

I will love my crosses, lifting my spirit above all of them, accepting equally joys as well as sorrows, health as well as sickness, light as well as darkness.

+ Jesus, I pray for priests of religious orders, so that You will be *everything* in their lives.

+ May families realize that life and all its benefits are a gift from You.

---

[11] Jn 1:11.

3

I Am the Resurrection and the Life

(Jn 11:25)

> Jesus, conqueror of death, comes
> to those who have died many
> deaths on account of sin to remind
> them that whoever lives in Him
> will not die again.

"Whoever believes in Me, even though he dies will live and all who live and believe in Me will never die."[12]

Have you heard? *"I am the Resurrection and the Life."* Be not afraid for *"whoever believes in Me,"* goes from death to divine life, the life of grace that only the Holy Spirit infuses.

Let your faith come alive and you will rise from the dead, because *I give life to those I want* and *I want to give it to you abundantly.*[13] Open yourself to receive this life. Come out of the sepulchre of your sins, *arise and walk*[14]; *come and follow Me.*[15]

Leave the old man in you, drink a new life of purity, holiness and love in My Blood. In Me, Who brought forth from nothing everything that is, Who is in Himself the fruitful beginning of all creation, *"there is life and the life is light for all men."*[16]

---

12 Jn 11:25-26.
13 Cf. Jn 10:10.
14 Cf. Jn 11:43-44.
15 Cf. Mt 19:21; Mk 10:21; Lk 18:22.
16 Jn 1:3-4.

Come to life and inhale this life of love that I am. Eat, drink and fill your heart with Him, Who is Life, Who came to give you *"life in abundance,"* [17] the Divine Word Who became Flesh to sacrifice Himself on the Cross and, in this way prove His Love, taking on a human Heart with which to suffer, and which trembles and palpitates in rhythm with your own.

I am He Who is to come [18] to take you to heaven, if you are fruitful, if you fulfill My commandment of love, if you are obedient and poor, if you are meek and humble of heart, if you love the cross and let yourself be crucified by God and men. Yes, do all this, because that is why I came to you, as Strength to your weakness, as Victor in your inconstancy and as a Focus of eternal life!

Act of Thanksgiving

Who am I that the Resurrection and Life should come to me? What shall I give You, Lord, in my littleness and nothingness and from the sepulchre of my great wretchedness? O, my good Jesus! May Your will be done, not mine, in all!

Receive me now with all my senses and powers: soul, heart, feelings and all that I have received from You, my dreams and my eternity, my past and my present, my joys and my sorrows, my agony and my death, so that You may convert them into Life!

I believe, my Lord and my God! I believe that even though I might be dead, I will live eternally; that temporal death will be for my body the passing into eternity. I believe that in the Eucharist I eat and drink the source of immortality and that the

---

[17]   Jn 10:10.
[18]   Rv 1:4.

more I become purified by Your contact, the more this earthly body will shine eternally on the day of the resurrection of the dead!

Erase my moments that are not Your moments, uproot from me all that is not You. I want my life to be Your life.

O, Mary, my life, my sweetness and my hope!, shake the wings of my poor heart so that leaving below the death of my falls, I will rise and fly to heaven, after practicing all the virtues of a supernatural and divine life.

Thoughts and Life

We should remember often that Jesus is *the resurrection and the life.*

The soul's clear light is the light of eternity. It is essential that we be alert and not fall asleep because we do not know the day or the hour.

Commitment

Jesus, my Life, by trying to practice some virtue with constancy, today I will build up treasure for heaven that *will always be.*

+ I offer to You today, Lord, all my good works for deceased priests.

+ Lord, increase in families hope in the true life.

4

I Am the Good Shepherd
(Jn 10:11, 14)

> Jesus, the Good Shepherd, leaves
> ninety-nine sheep to follow me, put
> me on His shoulders and free me
> from evil.

Yes, *I am the Good Shepherd*, the gentle and tender Shepherd Who throws Himself even among thorns to look for a lost sheep, Who loves His sheep very deeply and is delighted when He finds a lost one. I feed My beloved little sheep with My own Body and Blood, and I weep and sigh and stay awake calling them with loving whistles among the briar patches of the world.

This is your Jesus Who is looking for you, Who loves you. For years He has not lost sight of you and comes after you to make you happy, to heal your wounds, to carry you on His shoulders, to take you to the heavenly Father.

How may times I have taken you from the jaws of the wolf ready to devour you! What would you have done had My feet not run to search you out, if I had let you die? I am your Savior, the Good Shepherd. My eyes have cried over your lost ways, My feet have been wounded searching for you. Day and night My heart palpitates for you. My love for you is more than that of a father, more than that of a mother, more than that of friends, brothers, sisters and spouses.

Be not afraid, My little sheep, since I am your Shepherd,

your strength, your physician, your warmth, your consolation and even your food itself. Come, because I want to feel you at My side, resting on My shoulder. I want to hear the beating of your heart, to listen to your breathing, your panting for My Love. Come to My side and become white in My Blood that purifies everything it touches. *I am the Good Shepherd*, the Good Shepherd Who covers My beauty with sacramental veils, in order not to dazzle you.

"I know My sheep and My sheep know Me,"[19] This is why you and I have met! Therefore, come, the moment to make you happy has arrived. Come to inebriate yourself with the Blood of the Lamb. Come to be fed with the wheat of the chosen, with My Life itself that I give for My sheep. Come, My poor, weak and wounded little sheep. Come and receive the bread of the strong. Come, come!

Act of Thanksgiving

Jesus, *"You know Your sheep and Your sheep know You!"*[20] This is why I know You, because I am Yours. This is why I love You and I want also to give my life for You.

Jesus, on knowing You, we love You. *"The true [eternal] Life is this — to know You."*[21]

Good Jesus, kind, meek, humble, generous, mild, grateful, compassionate, thrice holy and a thousand times father, Good Shepherd, Glory of the Father.

"But I have other sheep," You said, *"who are not of this fold. I must lead them too, and they shall listen to My voice, and there shall be*

---

19 Jn 10:14.
20 Cf. Jn 10:14.
21 Cf. Jn 17:3.

one flock only and one Shepherd."[22] These words strike home to-day as I receive You in my innermost being and I offer, Lord, even though I am worth nothing, to sacrifice myself for You. Yes, my God, Good Shepherd, may they soon listen to Your voice! Bring them into the fold. May your Church triumph by the Holy Spirit, may the Cross reign, may Mary rule, and may we all form the fold that You came to unite on earth.

O, Mary, may we all know Jesus, the Good Shepherd! Grant us the grace to cooperate in the salvation of all for the glory of God and the unity of the Church.

Thoughts and Life

We should remember the words of Jesus *"The Father loves Me for this: that I lay down My life to take it up again. No one takes it from Me. I lay it down freely. I have power to lay it down, and I have power to take it up again. This command I received from My Father."*[23]

Commitment

Lord, give me strength to spend it for the good of all those around me, showing them Your kindness through my devotion and sacrifice.

+ Lord, I will offer You today many acts of kindness and sacrifice for all the archbishops and bishops, shepherds of the Church.

+ Jesus, Good Shepherd, may all families trust always in You.

---

22 Jn 10:16.
23 Jn 10:17-18.

5

I Am the Vine, You are the Branches
(Jn 15:5)

Jesus, the true Vine, comes to the branch that wishes to remain united to Him in order to communicate eternal life.

Listen to Me: *"I am the vine, you are the branches. He who lives in Me and I in him will bear much fruit for apart from Me you can do nothing."*[24]

You are My branch. You will give much fruit if you live from now on a life of intimacy with Me Who gave up My life for you on the cross. The Fountain of all good, my own Blood will run in your veins.

"Anyone who does not remain in Me will be thrown out like a branch and wither; people will gather them up and throw them into a fire and they will be burned. If you remain in Me and My words remain in you, you may ask for whatever you want and it will be done for you."[25] This is the great secret for union with Me, *to remain in My love, persevering until the end.* This was the essence of My advice on that night during which I instituted the Sacrament of Love to unite you to Myself.

Remain does not mean to stop at a point, but to be acti-

---

[24] Jn 15:5.
[25] Jn 15:6-7.

vated by a love that is always growing, burning and invading all, tending to develop unto the infinite.

The love of the Vine flows through the soul in the Eucharist and causes it to *come out of itself.* This love tends towards sacrifice as the butterfly towards the light, because the heart that is united to the true Vine is not satisfied with a sensible love or by words. Rather, drinking charity from My Heart, it is eager to give itself without measure, as I gave Myself. These are the effects of My intimate communication with the soul.

"My Father is the Grower of this Vine which is Me."[26] Love Him and be merciful as He is. To the Holy Spirit, the Sanctifier, ask that He come to unite your heart tightly to Mine, so that as a result of this *"My Father will be glorified in your bearing much fruit and being My disciples."*[27]

Ask my Holy Mother to open your heart and take you by the hand, to expand your desires and teach you to remain in Me.

Act of Thanksgiving

May You, my Jesus, be my peace, joy, rest and the only treasure of my life! I want, like the branch, to receive from You the Divine sap and grow with Your own substance that engenders purity. Communicate to me Your heavenly life and I will grow under Your shade, more intimately attached to You than the ivy to the tree. May Your Blood circulate through all my being.

My Mother, obtain for me the grace to remain in Jesus so that *the Father will grant me what I request,*[28] according to the prom-

---

[26] Cf. Jn 15:1.

[27] Jn 15:8.

[28] Cf. Jn 15:7.

ises of your Divine Son. And what shall I ask? To love Him always with a growing ardor in each moment of my life. And I will ask Him the grace to live in the world *doing good works as He did.*[29]

Thoughts and Life

> "While you look at Me, you will love Me.
> While you look at Me, you will imitate Me.
> While you look at Me, you will follow Me."

Commitment

Jesus, I open myself to receive Your Life. I want to remain in You.

+ Lord, today I offer You not to lose sight of Your very lively presence, for all diocesan priests.

+ Jesus, may united families have life in You.

---

[29] Acts 10:38.

6

It Is I, Be Not Afraid
(Mt 14:27)

> Jesus, Who commands the winds
> and they obey Him, comes to those
> who are weak in faith and fearful to
> give them courage and inspire them
> with total confidence in Him!

"Take courage! It is I. Do not be afraid," I said to My disciples, frightened to see Me early in the morning coming to them over the waters of the sea. What consoling words I say to you now from the Eucharist!

"It is I…." With Me and at My side, what can you fear? Whoever has Me possesses heaven because I am the God of Peace Who wishes to keep you safe. I am the God of forgiveness, Who loves you with a love that has no beginning, Who existed before the dawn of time and Who *"does not wish the death of the wicked… but rather rejoices when he turns from his evil ways that he may live."*[30]

I am Jesus, hidden in the Eucharist. I am the One performing miracles of omnipotence and power. I am here wishing to possess the whole of your person. Listen then with the ears of your soul to My voice that says: Be not afraid, throw yourself in the ocean of myrrh without hesitation because I am here. I will sustain you, if you have faith.

---

[30] Ezk 18:23.

I love you and therefore I come to you. You will fight against the winds of your passions in vain, if I am not at your side. I am He Who commands the oceans and calms tempests, as well as I calm the tempests of the hearts that come in search of Me and open their doors because they are Mine.

Do not tremble, be not afraid, I am your loving Jesus. Have faith and come without fear to the arms of My Mother, to this altar from whence My eyes search for you among the crowds. Come! Come! It is I, *I am.*

Act of Thanksgiving

O good Jesus, as St. Peter threw himself into the water without fear of coming to You when he heard You say, *"Come,"*[31] so I approach You with all the enthusiasm and energy of my being, sure of not sinking so long as I have faith.

"If it is really You, tell me to come to You."[32] Support me, Lord, and save me if I begin to sink once more in the bottomless sea of my own misery. It is true that "I cannot go to You without You," therefore stretch out Your hand, hold my arm as You did that of St. Peter and increase my faith in Your power and protection.

Jesus, my own Jesus, I love You and I am not afraid, because *You forgive much to the one who loves much.*[33] *"Create in me a clean heart!"*[34]

You are my strength. Look at me, Lord and expand my whole being to receive this increase of Divine Life.

---

[31] Cf. Mt 14:29.
[32] Mt 14:28.
[33] Cf. Lk 7:47.
[34] Ps 50:12.

Jesus, increase my faith and fill me with the confidence that makes easy the way of the Cross, lightens duties and is the privilege of the children of God. I cast my fears into the bosom of Your mercy because *no one who has hope in You will ever be put to shame.*[35]

You know, O Mother most clement, that I am weak and can do nothing by myself. But *He* has come to me. *He* has told me not to be afraid. Ask Him to bless me and to grant me the favor of always doing His Will.

Thoughts and Life

I will pay attention to this beautiful thought: *to do well whatever I do,* because it is what God wants of me today. And, how? Without fear of the difficulties, with a pure intention, with promptitude and joy.

Commitment

You call me today and I am not afraid, Jesus. You say that *it is You* and I do not hesitate to throw myself into any tribulation, assured that You are with me.

+ Jesus, today I offer You my intention to practice constantly some virtue for all the Church.

+ I ask You, Lord, that families increase their trust in You.

---

[35] Cf. Ps 24:2.

7

I Who Speak to You Am He

(Jn 4:26)

As He did at the well of Jacob to the
Samaritan woman, Jesus comes
close to the blind who do not
see the gift of God to make them
know Who He is.

At noon I was talking with the Samaritan woman. The hour of grace rang for her and she said to Me at the well of Jacob: *"I know there is a Messiah coming,"* and I said: *"I Who speak to you am He."*[36] Her heart was enlightened with grace and through My Humanity she recognized My Divinity and adored it filled with love and hope.

I am also the One Who speaks to you today. I have looked for you to the point of exhaustion in the highways and byways of the world. It is your Jesus, Who comes close to you in this consecrated Host.

I am He Who comes to ask, as I asked the Samaritan woman, *to give Me to drink* a little of the water of your contrition and your tears to quench My thirst. Your Jesus asks for this small alms. Will you deny it?

If you would only recognize the gift of God! If you could understand My predilection for you. If you were only able to

---

[36]   Jn 4:25-26.

comprehend the infinite love with which I follow you everywhere. If you could see My fervent desire to do you good. If you could see with your eyes the mountain of graces that I have bought with My Blood and that hang over you, longing for you to open your heart to receive them. If you would only appreciate My Cross, the secrets that it hides and the delights that God has reserved for the moment that you embrace them with love. If you could understand Who it is Who says to you: *Give Me to drink.*

Listen! Hear! This is the hour of your salvation. I am the One Who speaks, Who wants to pardon you, Who comes to you with all the tenderness of your Savior. Come! I am here!

Act of Thanksgiving

Jesus, my Redeemer and my hope: *"Speak, Lord, for Your servant is listening."*[37] *"You have the words of everlasting life."*[38]

You are the One Who speaks to my heart with the language of love, with the unknown language of the Cross that contains so much joy. Who will be able to separate me from You? *"Your delight is to be with the children of men."*[39]

Because of my weakness and misery, humiliation is painful, obedience is heavy, recollection is sad, temptation is intolerable, suffering is disturbing, and any cross is tiresome. I am afraid to forego my desires. Any kind of denial frightens me, but O my Jesus, I will be able to do all in union with You. Take away my coldness and give me the gift of prayer to listen to Your voice that encourages me to give of myself for love of You.

---

[37] Cf. 1 S 3:10.
[38] Jn 6:68.
[39] Cf. Pr 8:31.

Speak to me always, Jesus, Infinite Goodness and tell me, as You told the Samaritan woman, *everything that I have done* in order to move my heart to repentance!

Give me the water of Your Blood to cleanse my heart. Lord, give me this water!

Mary, Mother of the eternal Word, may I know how to listen in silence to the sweet voice of your Jesus. Amen.

Thoughts and Life

"Are you at peace? Pray, prayer will keep you there.
Are you tempted? Pray, prayer will sustain you.
Have you fallen? Pray, prayer will raise you up.
Are you discouraged? Pray, prayer will comfort you."

Commitment

Jesus, I will be attentive to Your voice today, I will not lose sight of You.

+ Lord, I ask You for priests in need.

+ Lord, may families listen to Your voice and believe in You.

8

I Am in the Father and the Father Is in Me
(Jn 14:11)

> Jesus, incarnate Word, equal to the
> Father and the Holy Spirit, comes
> to His creatures to manifest His
> infinite love.

"Do you not believe that I am in the Father and the Father is in Me? The words that I speak are not from Me.... It is the Father Who lives in Me accomplishing the works that I do."[40]

There is a Divine fruitfulness in the very heart of God, in His very pure essence, in the most intimate part of His being. God is happy, happiness itself.

In the eternity of perfections, which is *Divinity itself*, is born the Word, *"He Who already was in the beginning."*[41]

The Father begets the Word with all His perfections: Power, Beauty, Light and Life... and since They are two distinct Persons, there is a mutual pleasure, a joy, a union of intense love from which proceeds the third Divine Person, the Holy Spirit.

The bond of union and communication between the Father and the Son is the Holy Spirit. It is so beautiful, so perfect and so pure a unity that it cannot be understood on earth, since God alone is capable of understanding Himself in an absolute manner.

---

[40] Jn 14:10-11.
[41] Cf. Jn 1:1.

This Divine unity is the delight of the saints, the purity of the angels, and all the love of the blessed. It is the enchantment of heaven and of the Church on earth. Contemplate the identity that there is between the Father and Me: *I am in the Father and the Father is in Me!*[42]

That is why in honoring Me, you honor the Father and the Holy Spirit. Love Them as you love Me, by keeping My commandments.

I am the Word made flesh Who *"loves you with a love that had no beginning,"*[43] before the dawn of time, and Who came to expiate your sins before My heavenly Father, erasing them with the satisfaction of God humbled before God.

My love did not end there. I remained in the Eucharistic Sacrament, hiding My power, My greatness and My splendor to come to your heart, moving, purifying and saving it.

Come, cast yourself into the love of your God! Be not afraid. Come, I am waiting for you.

Act of Thanksgiving

Jesus, I believe that *You are in the Father and the Father is in You.* Teach me to live in filial confidence as a true child of the Father.

Jesus made man to erase my sins, You, Who are God with the Father and the Holy Spirit, took human nature in the womb of Mary to be able to love us with the infinite love of God as well as with a human love. I needed a God Who loved me as I love, Who loved me my way and *"the Word became Flesh,"*[44] that is to say, became man like me.

---

[42] Jn 14:11.
[43] Cf. 1 Jn 4:19.
[44] Jn 1:14.

Thank You, Jesus, because You knew man's need, therefore You became Man and became Eucharist. Thank You because, *being Who You are*, You lowered Yourself so that I could see You at all times, feel You close to me, visit You, entrust You with my sorrows and my joys and unite myself to You in the Eucharist. Here I feel You, I touch You. Here You are!

Be my teacher in the school of love. Teach me to know You, because if I know You, I know the Father. *"Whoever has seen Me, has seen the Father,"*[45] You said, and I want to fall into that abyss and immerse myself in that communion of Persons, in that unity of infinite perfections.

My Mother, you contemplate the mysteries of God face to face. Increase my faith and hunger for Jesus, infinite good.

Thoughts and Life

To make many acts of living faith in our heart, because our Father, joy, glory, honor and peace is there.

Let us, without rest, love Him Who is Love and be good, since goodness is something that has more from God than from man.

Commitment

What shall I do, Lord, to correspond in my littleness to Your kindness? I already know: to do the will of others before my own, to abandon myself to Your will, loving always my present situation, be it what it may.

+ Lord Jesus, I will make today many acts of hope in favor of the Church.

+ Father, Son and Holy Spirit, may families appreciate the grace of baptism that makes us living temples of the Trinity.

---

[45] Jn 14:9.

9

I Am the Light of the World
(Jn 8:12)

Jesus, God from God, Light from
Light, splendor of the Father, comes
to those who need light to illuminate
their desert with the light of eternal
life and to show them the way of the
Cross.

"I am the Light of the world. Whoever follows Me does not walk in darkness, but will have the light of life."[46] He will live in the truth and will be far away from the darkness of error and lies.

Light, light! What would you do without Me Who am the Light, that Light that shines in you through grace, as a star of first magnitude and as a thousand suns in the Eucharist?

I am the Light that illumines the most secret parts of the conscience, the eternal Light, the uncreated Light, Light from Light Who proceeds from the Father, *"Who enlightens every man who comes to this world."*[47]

I am Jesus-Eucharist, Who comes to dispel the night of your spirit; I want to flood your misery with My light. *I want you to see* and in order to see you need the Sun of Justice to dawn in you and give light to your eyes with the candor of the Eternal

---

[46] Jn 8:12.
[47] Jn 1:9.

Light. I, Who gave light to so many blind persons, want to heal the eyes of your soul, for you to know Me and remain in Me.

It is true that you have fled from Him Who is the Light, but it is also true that you look for Me, call out to Me and come to Me even with groping. You believe in My infinite love. You want to be healed and I never reject a contrite and humble heart. Come close then with love, with full confidence in the Light of Life.

Act of Thanksgiving

Jesus-Light, glory of the Father, thank You for coming to this place of exile to communicate Your love. Your love is so great that You wish to possess us eternally, inundating us with Your infinite Light.

You want to melt Your Heart into mine and unite Your Body, Blood, Light and Love to all my being. *"Father, I ask You, may they be one as We are one. I in them and You in Me, so that they may be perfectly one."*[48] Can there be a greater love?

Jesus, light of my existence, I want to follow You and be an image of Your life and abnegation. I want to love my brethren, sacrificing myself for them only to give You glory.

Lord, convert my soul into light in order that without any hindrance I will be united to Your light by such perfect compenetration as Fire to fire, Flame to flame, Light to light.

Jesus, my words do not express what I want to say, but You know how to listen to the silent language of love. I want to open myself to Your graces, wrapped in the light of Your splendors, hidden in the Eucharist.

---

[48] Jn 17:22-23.

Mary, Mother of Him Who is Light, give me great purity of conscience that from now on I will love, adore and be grateful to Jesus-Eucharist.

Thoughts and Life

Near Jesus-Eucharist I will continue to be joyful and at peace even in the midst of life's difficulties.

Commitment

Lord Jesus, today I will live under the light of Your Word that says: *"Once you were darkness, but now you are light in the Lord. Live, then, as children of the light. The fruit of light is to be found in every kind of goodness, justice and truth."*[49]

+ Jesus-Son, I will offer today many acts of love for religious teaching communities.

+ Jesus-Light, may families be open to You Who are the joy and happiness of hearts.

---

[49] Eph 5:8-9.

10

I Am the Bread of Life
(Jn 6:48)

> Jesus Who transforms the bread
> and wine into His Body and Blood
> comes to the weak to feed them and
> give them His own life.

"I am the Bread of Life. Whoever comes to Me will not hunger, and whoever believes in Me will not thirst."[50] These words speak to you of infinite humility and love without end, pronounced more by My Heart, which is an abyss of kindness, than by My lips.

Bread of Life, that is immortal food, divine substance that will strengthen you to reach your homeland without dying on the way. *"He who eats My Flesh and drinks My Blood has eternal life,"*[51] and this life is the true life, the life of grace that never dies, the immortal life that lasts for ever.

The Eucharist has the power of converting you into Me. If you could only understand the gift of God. I am the Bread of Life come down from heaven purely out of love!

My Flesh and My Blood will give you strength for the battles of life and will communicate to you the celestial fortitude that makes martyrs sacrifice themselves for love.

---

[50] Jn 6:35.
[51] Jn 6:54.

I want to live in you, so that you may live in Me in a divine transformation. I said to My heavenly Father, "*I am in them and You are always in Me, so that they may be brought to perfection as one,*"[52] because through this intimacy I want to communicate Myself to you. And these will be the effects of the *Bread of Life:* you will live united, permeated by your Jesus, one with the Father and the Holy Spirit.

Come, receive this Bread of love that costs nothing. "*It comes without cost,*"[53] because it is enough to have purity of heart to come to the Eucharist. Come, "*I Myself am the living Bread that has come down from heaven.*"[54]

Act of Thanksgiving

Lord Jesus, I live in You because You said: "*As I live because of the Father, so whoever feeds on Me will live because of Me.*"[55] I feel Your divine life flowing through my veins. I experience the fortitude of the martyrs to embrace any cross. *I am not afraid because for me life means Christ,*[56] *and Christ is living in me.*[57] In me is the Eucharistic seed of resurrection and life.

Jesus, You gave Yourself the name of Bread, the most common of all food for the poor and the rich, the children and the elderly and at the same time the most adequate for You, kind God. Your power is infinite and in the excess of Your love, You give Yourself to do good.

---

[52] Jn 17:23.
[53] Is 55:1.
[54] Jn 6:51.
[55] Jn 6:57.
[56] Ph 1:21.
[57] Gal 2:20.

I am weak, but You are my strength. I have no virtues but *You have them all* and will communicate them to me one by one, if I am faithful. *"I am able to do everything through the One Who strengthens me."*[58]

Remain in me and give me an intense continuous love that unites myself to You. O Jesus, *give me this Bread always!*

Virgin Mary, mother of the Bread of Life, may I never lack this Bread of the Eucharist. Amen.

Thoughts and Life

My Jesus, give me everyday some work, some suffering and some good to do.

To give only to give without paying attention to rewards, because love is *to give oneself,* to live *giving ourselves* to God and our neighbor in generosity.

Commitment

Jesus, You give Yourself. Make me capable of giving myself with You to those around me, being everything to everyone.

+ Lord, I offer you many acts of detachment in favor of the Church.

+ Jesus, increase in families the love of the Eucharist and feed them always with this heavenly Bread.

---

[58] Ph 4:13.

11

I Am Gentle and Humble of Heart
(Mt 11:29)

> Jesus, out of love, comes to the
> proud and oversensitive to intro-
> duce them into His Heart.

"Learn from Me, for I am gentle and humble of Heart." I do not come to teach science or ostentatious victories. I come to teach patience and humility. I want you to resemble your Jesus in this, *"who never breaks a bruised reed, nor quenches a smoldering wick."*[59] *"I went about doing good works,"*[60] and My Heart would break before any misfortune, pouring out treasures of love over the sick, the sorrowful and sinners.

"My Heart is moved with pity for the crowd,"[61] I said and I multiplied the bread in the desert. *"Son, do you want to be healed?"*[62] I asked the paralytic. I consoled, pardoned and loved making Myself everything to everyone. Because My time on earth was short, to satisfy the need to make hearts happy, I remained in the Eucharist, making Myself food for your love.

"Apart from Me you can do nothing,"[63] and that is why I am in the Eucharist, so that you may live in communion with Me.

---

[59] Mt 12:20.
[60] Acts 10:38.
[61] Mt 15:32.
[62] Jn 5:6.
[63] Jn 15:5.

Holy Communion not only takes away venial sins, but frees you from weaknesses and daily failures.

I am the strength of your weakness and I perform veritable miracles of love in those who receive Me, communicating strength and vigor for their sanctity. Come to this complete communion between the Creator and the creature, between two beings who look for each other, find each other and place in common all that they have and all that they are.

The power of union with Me is easy to attain. Simply approach Me with the purity and humility of a beloved disciple of Mine. For those who love, the only thing necessary is that they humble and lose themselves in the Heart of God.

Are you listening, you whom I love so much? What do you want that you cannot find in Me? Come and tell Me that you want to be healed so that I may give you health; that you repent of your sins so that I may pardon them; so *that you might love Me.* Yes, that you might love Me! And that is enough for Me to come to you, wiping away your tears and uniting your whole being to Mine.

Act of Thanksgiving

Heart of Jesus, make my heart like unto Yours! Communicate to me Your meekness and humility.

You came to light a fire on the earth,[64] and what do You want but that the world be inflamed in charity?

Jesus, I ask You that all the beatings of my heart and my affections be like Yours. Give me strength to suffer with patience and humility, to collaborate thus in the salvation of my brothers and sisters.

---

[64] Cf. Lk 12:49.

O Mary, gracious, sweet and loving mother! Obtain for me from Jesus that He pour out on me all the blessings that He sends to the world from the Eucharist, so that I might be a reflection of His meekness and humility.

Thoughts and Life

Hatred is cold and it freezes. When you are angry, count to ten before you speak and when you are in a rage count to one hundred.

Nothing is propagated faster among the members of a community or family than coldness, indifference and discouragement.

Commitment

Jesus, today I will conquer myself so that I might be meek and humble of heart, full of love and joy.

+ Jesus, I offer You today many acts of patience for diocesan priests.

+ Jesus, may families live in the light of Your Word.

12

I Testify on My Behalf and the Spirit Will Bear Witness in My Behalf

(Jn 8:18; 15:26)

Jesus, the Savior sent by the Father comes to those who want to know Him and love Him, to tell them that He will pray to the Father and will send them another Consoler.

"I testify on My behalf and so does the Father Who sent Me." [65]

"The Spirit of Truth Who proceeds from the Father and Whom I Myself will send together with the Father will bear witness on My behalf." [66]

All the Trinity gives testimony about Me: the Father, the Holy Spirit and I Myself, the Word bear witness to My Divinity. *"And you as well,"* I said to My disciples, *"will bear witness because you have been with Me from the beginning."* [67]

For the sake of clarity, I said: *"I will ask the Father and He will give you another Paraclete to be with you always."* [68] *"The Paraclete, the Holy Spirit Whom the Father will send in My Name will teach you everything and remind you of all that I have told you."* [69]

---

[65] Jn 8:18.

[66] Jn 15:26.

[67] Jn 15:27.

[68] Jn 14:16.

[69] Jn 14:26.

Here is the secret. If you want to remember My Word, that is I Myself, the Word, in the Gospel, then come to the Holy Spirit and He will enlighten your mind. He will teach you what you do not know, open the ears of your spirit and move your will, making His dwelling in your heart.

The Holy Spirit will come to you as a fruit of My prayer. I asked the Father to send Him to you. He is the light that illumines, the fire that warms, the breath that gives life.

The Holy Spirit is the soul of the Church. He lives in My Heart and in the Eucharist.

The Holy Spirit unites Me to souls. He is the Strength of God, the unfailing Light, Who helps My Church with His infallible Truth, and the Author of all My grace.

People look for other means to halt impiety, preserve the faith, remedy evils, and they forget the *principal means*, since only the Holy Spirit can renew the face of the earth and give witness to the Word made Flesh.

By the Holy Spirit, I was conceived in Mary. Through Him I offer Myself as a Victim without blemish. He is spiritual perfection, the sun of the spirits, the bond that unites you to Me, the joy of hearts, the repose of souls. By Him prophets were taught, priests are ordained, altars are consecrated, the Church is sanctified, demons are expelled and souls healed.

If you wish to be healed, the Holy Spirit is a doctor. If you are poor, He is your Father. He is warmth, refreshment, Life.

Love this Holy Spirit with all your heart and you will receive communion with fervor. Keep Him always in you and you will not sin. He is the pledge of glory. Ask Him to remind you of your Jesus.

Ask the Holy Spirit, Who loves the Word as much as the Father, to teach you the essence of love. He wants to pour forth

His gifts and fruits and finds no recipient to receive them. Do not sadden Him and keep your conscience pure.

My Heart suffers to see that the Holy Spirit is almost unknown in the world. Extend His devotion, His reign. He is the axis of all that is pure and holy.

You also, as My disciple, must bear witness on My behalf and you will do it by loving and making the Father and the Spirit of Love loved.

Come to Me that I may give you My own Holy Spirit! Come!

Act of Thanksgiving

Jesus-Eucharist, give me Your Holy Spirit. I want to be His living temple so that He might live in me. Ask Him to penetrate my mind, so that Your Light will reign there. Ask Him to absorb my will so that in it the sanctity of Your Heart will radiate. May He reign in all my being, all my actions, words and thoughts so that I may live *a divine life,* doing always Your Will. I want Him to be my Director, my Guide, my Consoler, my Strength so that I may sacrifice myself with joy in any cross.

"The Love of God has been poured out into our hearts by the Holy Spirit,"[70] and makes easy by grace what is difficult by nature. He enables us to value rightly the things of this earth and helps the soul aspire to the things of heaven. Therefore fill me with Your beneficial influence, my good Jesus, equal in all things to the Father and this Divine Spirit.

Mary, Spouse of the Holy Spirit, ask Him to come and reign throughout the whole world, to send apostles who are on fire to extend His devotion and make it loved, because who

---

[70] Rm 5:5.

ever is possessed by His anointing, will love the Cross, the Word as well as the Father, and you, Queen of the Apostles.

Holy Spirit, mysterious and Divine fire that gives life to all You touch, make me holy by the daily reception of the Body and Blood of Jesus and lift up my heart to heavenly desires. Amen.

Thoughts and Life

Those who have the Holy Spirit will never be proud and are convinced of their own misery. They will live with their eyes fixed on heaven without forgetting their duties on earth.

May the Holy Spirit, fountain of all purity, communicate that purity to us by means of the cross and keep our bodies and souls ever pure and without blemish.

Commitment

Holy Spirit, I will spread Your devotion by whatever means are possible and I will see everything clearly through Your divine influence.

+ Holy Spirit, I pray to You for the Shepherds of the Church.

+ Jesus, grant us by the action of the Holy Spirit that families give witness to You in the world.

13

I Am the Way
(Jn 14:6)

Jesus, the Way, comes to those who
look for Him to take them by the
hand to the Father's house.

"I am the way.... No one goes to the Father except through Me."[71]

I am the Way and I come to you in the Eucharist, that is,
the way that you look for in the darkness, a sure way although
full of thorns.

Do you want to take this road, do you want to follow Me?
*"Whoever wishes to come after Me must deny his very self, take up his
cross and follow in My footsteps."*[72]

Does this frighten you? Is it not a joy to suffer for those
whom you love? Nothing can be called a sacrifice in the language
of love. For to whomever lives in communion with Jesus-Eucharist, everything is possible. Walk towards Calvary and very
soon you will see yourself transformed because *"My yoke is
easy,"*[73] and the cross carries the one who bears it with love.

Be not afraid to enter this day through this Way which is
Myself. I will not abandon you. I will be your Cyrenean, cross-
ing the desert with you and carrying you in My arms. In the dark-

---

[71] Jn 14:6.
[72] Mt 16:24.
[73] Mt 11:30.

ness I will be your light; in danger, your security; in tempests, your tranquility; and in battle your stronghold.

I came to earth to teach sacrifice and all My life can be summed up in these words: immolation out of love! Come, then, to Me; open yourself to Me, so that I may come to you and you will find fortitude in your sufferings. Come to Me and through Me you will come to the Father and the Holy Spirit Who will be your joy for all eternity.

Act of Thanksgiving

Jesus, You are my Way and I will follow You, embracing the crosses that You wish to send to me, for love finds consolation when it suffers. I hear Your voice from the Cross saying to me, "Here I am." I want to direct my steps towards You. Calvary is the road of those who love, the only direct way to heaven.

Sweet Mother, who knows Jesus-Way and guides us to eternal glory, obtain for me the grace to follow Him until death, denying myself and embracing the cross.

Thoughts and Life

"Let us have full confidence of entrance into the sanctuary by virtue of the Blood of Jesus Who is our new and living Way."[74]

Commitment

Jesus, I will keep silent whenever I am annoyed and will not excuse myself today, in order to offer You the gift of self-forgetfulness and the abnegation that You alone can see.

+ Lord I offer You many acts of self-denial for missionaries.

+ Jesus, may You be the Way for all families.

---

[74]   Heb 10:19.

14

I Am the Truth

(Jn 14:6)

Jesus, the Truth, comes to those
who walk in darkness to give them
Himself, Who is Light and Truth.

"You know the way that leads where I go,"[75] I said confidentially to My disciples, announcing to them My departure. *"Lord, we do not know where You are going,"* Thomas replied. *"How can we know the way?"* *"I am the Way,"* I answered, *"and the Truth and the Life."*[76] I am the Way by My example, the Truth by My doctrine, and the Life by My grace.

I am the eternal Truth and *"for this reason I came into the world,"* I told Pilate and added, *"to testify to the Truth. Anyone committed to the truth hears My voice."*[77]

And you have heard My voice and belong to Me and that is the reason why I love you so much and I give you Myself: My Body, My Blood, My Soul and My very Life. *"Come to Me all of you."*[78] You heard and your feet ran to find Me and you opened your heart to My teachings. Faithful to My voice, you come close today to receive Me and at the same time to drink this Truth that gives light to your intelligence.

---

[75] Jn 14:4.
[76] Jn 14:5-6.
[77] Jn 18:37.
[78] Mt 11:28.

By essence, I am the Truth, and in the Truth are to be found all My attributes. I am the Eternal Truth, the Word of God, one with the Father, without past or future, united to the Father by the bond of love and light that is the Holy Spirit, being three Persons in one substance. In this eternal Truth are all the attributes of God which are no less than infinite Truth itself.

The Light is also enclosed in this Truth, because Truth is Light, an eternal Light without shadows and of an infinite clarity. You cannot understand this, because only God can understand this mystery.

The Truth includes the Life attributed to the Holy Spirit, Who with the Father is eternal fecundity and has the mission to bring forth Life, not only that which is material but also the life of grace, whose source is the Holy Spirit.

The life of grace grows to the extent to which the soul opens itself to receive it. When the soul cooperates, faithfully corresponding, the Holy Spirit pours Himself into the soul with showers of grace, torrents of light, enabling it to know, feel and love that infallible Truth, eternal Sun without shadows, Sea of mysteries that are clarified in that light of the Divinity.

Since I gave you a slight idea of this Truth which I am, I come today to you with all My richness and light to illumine your powers, divinizing them.

Come to drink from the very pure fountain of truth without error. Come, that it might bring light to your mind and help you distinguish gold from brass, true from false, what you are and what I am.

Be not afraid, you are Mine. *"I do not come to condemn you but to save you."*[79] I come to give witness to the Truth. Come

---

[79] Cf. Jn 3:17.

close. Be confident here is the Truth that can neither deceive nor be deceived. Come, be not afraid of your littleness, since I became the Bread of Life that I might come close to you!

Act of Thanksgiving

My Lord and my God, Eternal Truth, Light, Way, Truth and Life, known fully by God alone! I adore You, I bless You and I praise You without understanding You. *I believe* in Your Word of eternal life and recognize Your immensity and my nothingness.

Divine Word, You became man and unite Your Body, Soul and Divinity to the whole of my being by means of the Eucharist, in order to become one with me.

How can I repay You in my impotence for this insanity of love? What did You see in me, Sovereign Truth, that could attract You? The image of the Trinity which I bear is what made You come from heaven to take me to You.

Being God, You made Yourself food to come into me and there diffuse in my heart and mind that splendor of Truth, the glory of the Divine, the radiation of all the Trinity. You did not want any distance to exist between Your soul and mine.

Your love went to the ultimate limit. *You loved me to the end.*[80] In the Eucharist You are God *with* us and God *in* us, transforming us into You and making of two lives, one.

My Mother, you who know Jesus-Truth by the action of the Holy Spirit, uproot all errors from our minds, so that the light of Truth, that is Jesus, might penetrate into us and we might listen to His voice and follow Him.

---

[80] Cf. Jn 13:1.

Thoughts and Life

In order to listen to the voice of God, we need ears that are not attuned to the noise of the world and its passions. Let us not be inattentive to the voice of the Holy Spirit, because it contains infinite treasures of the love of Jesus, bought by His Blood. To disregard His inspirations is to snuff out this light and remain in darkness.

Commitment

Jesus, eternal Truth, I want to listen to Your voice in order to belong to You.

+ Jesus-Truth, I will offer many acts in response to Your love in favor of unbelievers who deny You.

+ Jesus, grant families to live in You Who are the Truth.

15

I Am the Life
(Jn 14:6)

> Jesus, true Life, uncreated, without
> beginning or end, comes to die for
> those who die to sin in order to
> communicate Life to them.

"I am the Life," supernatural, Divine, celestial life, the life of grace, true life as compared to earthly life that is but a shadow.

I have remained in the Eucharist to give you this Life, that is to give you Myself, Who am Life, because I want to live in you, in your faculties, your soul, the senses of your body, in each drop of your blood.

Stroke by stroke I want to imprint in your being My humility, zeal, obedience, abnegation, simplicity, patience and love of the cross.

"I have come that they might have life and have it to the full."[81] And what better way to communicate it than through Holy Communion? Therefore, drink, fill yourself with Him Who is Life.

My life, during My passage on earth, I translated into patience, simplicity and charity. *"I went about doing good work,"*[82] even though I was surrounded by hatred, criticism and the calumnies of My enemies.

---

[81] Jn 10:10.
[82] Acts 10:38.

Look and take in the silence and the power of the Eucharist, and reproduce Me in all your being. I want to put My living Heart in yours, and if you allow Me, to take away your bad dispositions and vices. It will no longer be you who live, but I will live in you a life of intimacy, through a Divine transformation on the part of the Holy Spirit living in you. Love with all your strength the Holy Spirit Who rules by love.

Sanctity is the fruit of constant acts of love. Therefore, love Me; actively remove whatever separates you from Me, creating a void; deny yourself by mortifications in order to be filled by Me.

Eat My Body, drink My Blood, satisfy your hunger for the divine by receiving the Way, the Truth and the Life. Each morning My Heart waits for you. Having *"Life in abundance"*[83] here, I do not want you to die. I have a love of predilection for you.

Come to Me in humility and trust, with an ardent love. Then contemplate, be silent, enjoy and admire, falling deep into the abyss of Myself and your nothingness.

Act of Thanksgiving

Jesus, give me Your love because whoever has no love, has no life and I want to live loving. I want to live inspired by the love and sacrifice that You teach me in the Eucharist. From Your cradle to Calvary and from Calvary until there is only one altar in the world, You will be a Victim, my very beloved Jesus, offering Yourself ceaselessly for men. So will I give myself for others without thinking about myself, making myself all things for all men and love will give me the strength.

---

[83] Cf. Jn 10:10.

I already feel this abundant life flowing through my veins. Lord, please grant me the grace to use all this life in favor of the Church, Your glory and the salvation of my neighbor.

I do not want any more rewards on earth but *the power to do good.* I ask You for *the grace to know how to sacrifice* myself for You in love.

Mary, good and heavenly Mother, who gave human life to the Eternal Life! I will not die if I live this life, my death being only a dream from which I will awaken in your arms. In the meantime, I ask you that, with each breath, you give me your Jesus united to your heart, so that I may pay Him homage.

Thoughts and Life

In difficulties with other people, to have *love;* with things, *prayer;* and with every wound that bleeds from my heart I will utter these words: *God wills it!* Whoever is truly united with God, should not have sorrows, occupations and sufferings that distract the mind from Him Who is the Life, Jesus.

Commitment

It is easy to say, "Lord, I love You," but if this is not accompanied by Christian mortification, it is vain and without foundation, since self-love would occupy everything in me.

+ Lord I will offer many acts of abandonment to Your Will for the peace of Your Church.

+ Jesus, please help families to value the gift of life and to defend it in dangerous circumstances, so that the civilization of love may reign.

16

I Did Tell You,
But You Do Not Believe That I Am
(Jn 10:25)

> Jesus, model of all virtues comes
> to those who need to see with the
> eyes of faith, to teach them to
> believe and love.

"How long are You going to keep us in suspense? If You really are the Christ tell us so in plain words,"[84] the Jews who gathered around Me said to Me one day.

"I did tell you, but you do not believe Me," I answered. *"The works I do in My Father's name give witness in My favor; but you do not believe because you are not My sheep. My sheep hear My voice, I know them and they follow Me. I give them eternal life and they shall never perish. No one shall snatch them out of My hands."*[85]

How many times I gave them to understand in a thousand ways My Divinity! To how many others did I clearly declare that I was the promised Messiah, the Principle of all things, The Way, the Truth and the Life, yet they closed their ears and their heart to My voice! *How often did I want to cover them with My wings, like a mother hen with her chickens, but they ran away from Me!*[86]

But you, if you follow Me, come to look for Me in the Eu-

---

[84] Jn 10:24.
[85] Jn 10:25-28.
[86] Cf. Lk 13:34.

charist, tell Me that you belong to Me, that you want to listen to My teachings, that you believe in the mysteries of My Divinity, even though you do not understand them, that all My works witness to you of the love of your magnanimous God Who *"takes no pleasure in the death of a wicked man but rather in the wicked man's conversion that he may live."*[87]

Blessed faith that makes saints! The most pleasing work for God is that *"we have faith in the One Whom He sent."*[88] *"Whoever believes in the Son shall have eternal life."*[89]

Believe, make your faith firm and *"no one shall snatch you out of My hands."*[90] *"The just one lives by faith."*[91]

To grow in the spirit of faith is your sanctification. This spirit consists in believing, living and doing all illuminated by faith, orienting nature's instincts towards this light: likes and dislikes, customs and aspirations, doing them for a supernatural purpose. May the presence and sense of God accompany you always.

The Eucharist is saying to you always: *"I Am"* Goodness, Tenderness, Love, Purity, your Redeemer, your Savior, the one you dream about at night and call upon during the day, your Companion, your Strength.

Open your heart because I want to possess it and teach you to look at everything in the light of faith and love.

Act of Thanksgiving

Jesus, Who is more worthy to be loved than You? Remove the veils that cover You from my sight and unite me to Yourself

---

[87] Ezk 33:11.
[88] Jn 6:29.
[89] Jn 6:40.
[90] Cf. Jn 10:28.
[91] Heb 10:38.

for ever. *"My life is Christ"*[92]; for this life, I was born and from this union follows the life that is both supernatural and divine. This union is my goal, my heaven, because heaven is the union of the creature with God. This present life is only a learning process to acquire degrees of union with You.

Jesus-Eucharist, You ardently desire this intimacy: it is the thirst that consumed You at the well with the Samaritan woman and again at the Cross. This love of Yours moves me, sustains me and communicates to me the secret of all the virtues.

Jesus, look at me at those moments with that penetrating Divine glance that pierces secrets and mysteries, that tears away the veil of conscience, that pierces hearts, that looks and keeps on looking, loving! I need to *know* this love, *feel* this love, *remember* this love, and the Eucharist is the communication through which Love itself moves into the heart that loves Him.

Mary, you who always saw God with the purity of your heart, increase my faith and purity of heart to see God in everything.

Thoughts and Life

A pure heart knows nothing but love because it possesses the fountain of love that is God.

When Jesus lives in me, my will is His.

Commitment

Jesus, grant that I may live with my eyes fixed on You, so that You teach me to see everything in the light of faith.

+ Lord, I offer You today many acts of faith for those who do not believe in You.

+ Jesus, increase in all families faith in You.

---

[92] Ph 1:21.

17

Unless You Believe That I Am, You Will Surely Die in Your Sin
(Jn 8:24)

> Jesus, the Lord, comes to the heart
> of those who wish to love Him to
> teach them the Gospel.

Teaching in the Temple, I said to the Jews, *"Unless you believe that I am, you will surely die in your sin."* But these words are not addressed to you. Thanks to My Father, you believe that *I am the Word made flesh*[93] Who came down from heaven to the virginal womb of Mary. I was born in a manger in extreme poverty. I fled to Egypt, and was subject to Joseph and My Holy Mother for thirty years. I worked hidden in a workshop, I visited towns doing good, healing, consoling, resurrecting the dead and being everything to everyone.

You believe that *I am* He Who agonized in the Garden of Olives, accepted the humiliating chalice of the Passion, was abandoned, betrayed, calumniated, accused, crowned with thorns, whipped and sentenced to death. You believe that I carried the Cross without complaint and was nailed to it. With Divine love and for the sake of My enemies, I died in frightful torment. You believe that I allowed a spear to pierce My Heart opening in it the door to heaven.

---

[93] Cf. Jn 1:14.

You believe that I am really present in the Eucharist and that there is not a single moment that My oblation on the altars ceases, glorifying My Father with My redemptive Blood that cleanses the crimes of the world.

Yes, you believe that *I am*, that I have done everything for the sake of men, and for this reason you will not die in your sin, because *he who believes in Me will be saved.*[94]

Come, receive the Lamb of God Who takes away the sins of the world! One single communion is sufficient to destroy defects, implant virtues and make saints. Do you not feel upon you the infinite tenderness of My glance which envelops you? Come close, *I am* Jesus, the *Fountain of happiness* Who wants to quench your thirst.

I want to be your consolation, your inseparable companion until I take you to the splendors of eternity, communicating to you the seed of the resurrection. *I am* the sure pledge of Life. Come, come.

Act of Thanksgiving

Jesus, the whole of my being, in Whom I *believe* and *hope* and *love* with all the strength of nature and grace, You are love, sweetness and kindness without end!

I believe that You are *"my Lord and my God."*[95] I believe everything that the Church teaches.

I do not want to die in my sin, Jesus, but to be saved by Your Blood. My soul is sorrowful for having offended You.

I give myself to You always, begging You to accept me as

---

[94]   Cf. Mk 16:16.
[95]   Jn 20:28.

I am. I do not know how to love, if You do not teach me. I do not know how to unite myself to You, if You do not unite me to Yourself. Only You are my way, my health, the breath of my weakness.

O Mary, always faithful to Jesus in all the stages of His life! Teach me abnegation and abandonment. Make me know Jesus more and more in order to imitate Him in His love without end. Amen.

Thoughts and Life

A great deal of our evil proceeds from our imagination, from the exaggerated idea that we have about ourselves and our worth, desiring to increase our place in the world.

Humility is truth. God is All and we are nothing and God loves us as small as we are.

Commitment

God, I want to make many acts of faith and good works in order *not to die in my sin*, because *faith without works is dead*.[96]

+ Lord, I offer You today many acts of faith, hope and charity for the intentions of the Pope and the propagation of the faith.

+ May families, Lord, believe in You and live in accordance with their faith.

---

[96] Jm 2:17.

18

You Address Me as Teacher and Fittingly Enough, For This is What I Am

(Jn 13:13)

> Jesus Teacher comes to His
> disciples to illuminate their minds
> with the light of Truth.

"You address Me as Teacher and fittingly enough, for this is what I am," I said one day to My disciples, and I repeat it to you. I am your Teacher; *"And this is My commandment: that you love one another as I have loved you."*[97] *"You will live in My love if you keep My commandments"*[98]; by this *"all will know that you are My disciples."*[99]

And how have I loved them? Not with words, but until death — death on the Cross; I taught everything by example: self-denial, love, sacrifice, mercy, etc. I invited you to follow Me, walking ahead and abandoning Myself to all the sacrifices of My Soul and Heart up to giving up My life for you. *"I have given you an example,"*[100] and *"no pupil outranks his teacher."*[101]

Follow the program of sanctity that I proposed to the young man in the Gospel, when he asked Me one day: *"Teacher, what*

---

[97] Jn 15:12.
[98] Jn 15:10.
[99] Jn 13:35.
[100] Jn 13:15.
[101] Mt 10:24.

must I do to obtain eternal life?" "Keep the commandments," I answered. *"I have kept all these from my youth,"* he replied. *"Never-*
theless, one thing is still lacking," I added. *"If you want to be perfect,*
go sell everything that you have and give to the poor. You will then have
treasures in heaven. Afterwards come back and follow Me."[102]

What do you say to all these teachings? Is your heart willing to follow this way of sanctity? Nothing is impossible for the
one who loves. Examine *what is still lacking* and put into practice virtues that are solid, loving Me with all your heart, with all
your soul, with all your strength and your neighbor in Me and
for Me as yourself.

"Whoever keeps My commandments loves Me and I will love him
and will reveal Myself to him."[103] Now if you want to follow Me
more closely, if you have a religious vocation, do not ignore it
since it is a pearl from heaven. Follow then My second coun-
sel, leave everything to unite yourself to Me.

I Myself am in the Eucharist and I will give you the su-
pernatural strength you need to put My teachings into practice.
Come close as My beloved disciple, drink from the fountain of
My Heart.

Act of Thanksgiving

Jesus, good Master, my Lord and my God, with what can
I repay You for the holy teachings that You have imparted to
me along with Your very Self? I praise You with my skills, sen-
timents, body, soul and all my being. I would like to spend my
whole life giving You thanks for Your teachings.

One thing is still lacking, You said to the young man in the

---

[102] Mt 19:16-21.
[103] Jn 14:21.

Gospel and I myself lack many things. I need humility, patience, the spirit of mortification, love for my neighbor and many other virtues. It will be known that I am Your disciple if I love my brothers and sisters with Your own love.

Mary, my Mother, obtain for me the grace to learn to love, profiting from the lessons of my Divine Teacher.

Thoughts and Life

A selfish spirit derives pleasure from being loved; a Christian heart, from loving without reward.

Can it be said in truth that one loves when nothing costly has been given?

Commitment

Lord, when I can not pardon the action, may I at least pardon the intention of my neighbor, and may I not always have the tiniest measure to give and the largest one to receive.

+ Jesus, may parents and teachers teach little children and young people to know You.

+ Lord, may families be schools of sanctity.

19

My Father and I Are One
(Jn 10:30)

Jesus, God and man, one
with the Father comes to His
limited poor creatures to reveal
to them His Divinity.

"My Father and I are one," I said to the Jews. *"If I do not perform My Father's work, put no faith in Me. If I do perform them, believe in the works, even if you do not believe in Me and thus you will know that the Father is in Me and I am in the Father."*[104] By My works you should realize that I am not only a man but God with all the power of the Father, power to forgive, to save, to heal, to resurrect and to do all the many wonders that I have performed on earth.

But they closed their eyes to the light of truth. They did not believe in Me or in My Father Who sent Me. They took stones to throw at Me. They wanted to capture Me and did not satisfy their hatred until they killed Me, nailing Me to the Cross.

Yes, you gaze upon this God of Love, *Whose very being is to give and communicate Himself.* He is one God in three Persons: Father, Son and Holy Spirit, Who gives Himself without being consumed in an eternity without time, in an immensity without limits, in a sea of perfections without bottom or sides, Joy in Joy itself, Love and Life in Life itself.

---

[104] Jn 10:37-38.

Yes, you do believe that *the Father and I are one*, and that the Incarnation, Redemption, the Church and the Eucharist and all that has been done has been done by the God-Man, by the Word made Flesh, inseparable from the Father and the Holy Spirit. Beautiful faith that will be rewarded by the possession of the Holy Trinity Itself! Receive Me, come close to receive in communion your God, the Word made Man for you. Look at Him. Listen how He calls you by your name. Come!

Act of Thanksgiving

Jesus, I take delight in seeing You alive in Your Holy Gospel. There, in those pages, is the Word to which the Holy Spirit gives life, echoing the Eternal Word. The Father is there in You. You are there in our midst, with Your holiness, kindness, mercy and love. There, as in the Eucharist, is *the Good Teacher*, the Good Shepherd, the Bread of Life, the Light of the World, the same Jesus Who *chose this new way to remain among us*.

Jesus, I beg You to make me know more and more the beloved Father, one with You, Who is in heaven and Who is "Our Father."

Ask Him to send workers into His vineyard, to extend His kingdom with that of the Cross, that is the Gospel, and the kingdom of sorrow and of love with devotion to the Holy Spirit. Tell Him that I only desire one thing intensely on earth, that His Will be done in me and in all His creatures.

Ask Him, my good Jesus, that there be no day in which He does not give me the Bread of Life, the Divine Victim as food.

Mary, my Mother, you who have heard all my petitions to the beloved Father, support them with your prayers. Amen.

Thoughts and Life

All comes from God, Who is my Father.

They will be saints in body and soul if the Gospel is on their lips and in their heart.

Commitment

Jesus, Son of the Father, I promise to read every day some verses of the Gospel, meditating on them and thus bringing to life in me the Spirit of the Son, Who is the Holy Spirit.

+ Lord, I offer to meditate today slowly on the Our Father in favor of all the members of schools and universities.

+ May unity reign in families, Lord, as a reflection of the Holy Trinity.

20

You Belong To What Is Below,
I Belong To What Is Above

(Jn 8:23)

> Jesus the Lord comes to His
> creatures, satisfied with the goods
> of earth, to show them the delights
> of the spiritual life.

"You belong to what is below, I belong to what is above," I said while I was on earth. Why did I come? I came to take you out of the misery in which you were and to raise you to the dignity of a child of God. I want to make you see that you are the masterpiece of My power.

The three Divine Persons have communicated to you a reflection of Their perfections, making you intelligent, free, spiritual, and active, an expression of Their greatness.

Love created you. You are the object of My affection, what I came in search of on earth and what I pursue with all the strength of My love in the Eucharist.

You are of earth, but you have a Savior Who is of heaven, Who came to unite these two poles with the powerful magnet of love, to purchase you with the price of His own life. Therefore you are worth more than all the wonders of the firmament and are superior to the stars, because *you are worth the very life of your Jesus,* Who is always ready to sacrifice His life for you.

For your good, at every moment on altars everywhere I ascend new calvaries and I am in the Eucharist ready to pour forth My graces on all men.

Have you occasionally considered these truths?

Love your life, a creation of love that has come from the Heart of God and should return there. Be an altar to receive Me and adore Me in every instant. *You are of earth*, it is true; but transformed in Me, *you will be of heaven.*

What would you do if at this moment you were asked, what have you done with your life? Come to be divinized by My touch. Leave your vices behind and curb your tendencies. From there ascend to Me to be My image, fully human and fully divine. Come.

Act of Thanksgiving

Jesus, I give You thanks with gratitude and love. Inclined to the things here below, I have ceased raising my eyes to that place where You dwell and that paradise of delights and joys that exceeds all human understanding: heaven!

You are from there, Jesus, made Eucharist to divinize me so that You can take me to enjoy Your companionship.

"You take no pleasure in the death of the wicked man, but rather in the wicked man's conversion and life." [105] Raise my eyes, my spirit and all my being so that I search for You, Infinite Good, in Whom is contained all good. Sorrows pass and the reward will be eternal. The trial is short and heaven is everlasting. There those who cry will be consoled, the clean of heart will be happy.

Take me with You and communicate to me Your likeness

---

[105] Ezk 33:11.

with the food of Your Blood and Your Body, transforming me in You, the Crucified. By receiving Communion every day, Your Father will receive me and then I will be from above.

Mary, you who lived on earth a heavenly and divine life, obtain for me the grace to live in the world doing my work with great purity of intention! Amen.

Thoughts and Life

If you wish God to listen to you, listen to Him.

Sanctity depends less on what we do than in the way we do it.

"You are worth as much as your prayer is worth," said St. John of the Cross.

Your life in God, God in your life.

My feet on earth but my heart in heaven.

Commitment

Jesus, may I not lose sight of You today and may I take time each day for prayer. This is the starting point of the interior life.

+ Lord, I will offer You today many spiritual communions in favor of communities and persons consecrated to God.

+ Jesus-Eucharist, may families cultivate the interior life to be close to You.

21

It Was Not You Who Chose Me, It Was I Who Chose You

(Jn 15:16)

Jesus comes to those He has
chosen to show them His love of
predilection.

One day when I was teaching My disciples the law of love,
I said: *"It was not you who chose Me, rather, it was I Who chose you…
so that whatever you ask the Father in My Name, He will give you."*[106]
And you are one of the children of My Heart's predilection.
Look back and count, if you can, all the graces that in My kind-
ness I have given you.

When you still were not, I had your name written in My
Heart. Many others would have served and loved Me better than
you, but *I had chosen you from all eternity*. And, I rejoiced in giving you being, in impregnating you with graces, in preparing for
you, through the Eucharistic banquet, a cross as a precious gift
of My affection.

I knew that your parents would die, but I would not leave
you orphans. When they died they left goods, but they could
not leave themselves. I can because I am all powerful and
infinite, and more loving than all parents. I give you My Body,
Soul and Divinity. Eat today this infinite Good because I only

---

[106] Jn 15:16.

want now to be one with you. *"My Flesh is real food and My Blood real drink. The man who eats My Flesh and drinks My Blood remains in Me and I in him."*[107]

I came into the world to be close to you. Therefore I came from heaven to take in Mary a Heart that would beat in rhythm with your own. That is why I suffered and died on the Cross to purchase for you the joy of reconciliation, to give you sacraments and in them My Heart to cleanse you from your sins. Therefore, finally, I am here in the Eucharist, as a miracle of omnipotence, hiding My splendor to adjust to the material of your heart.

You may lack in the world hearts that love you, but not Mine! You will always have Me on the altars, ready to wipe your tears, to listen to your confidences, to take My Heart from My bosom and place it into yours.

Then the happy moment of this union arrived. It is I Who chose you before you were.

Open your heart with humility, yes, but with holy enthusiasm. I have come to fill you in the most intimate part of your being. Come, come close!

Act of Thanksgiving

Jesus, it is true that I have not chosen You because I did not know You, but You had chosen me *even though You knew me*. Jesus, You chose me without my being worthy of it. What did You see in me, my Lord and my God? Misery and poverty that moved Your infinite love. Thank You, Jesus! I ask Mary to give me her lips to repeat: Thank You! *"Many are called but few are chosen."*[108] I trust in Your mercy in order never to leave You.

---

[107] Jn 6:55-56.
[108] Cf. Mt 22:14.

You said to those You had chosen that *whatever they asked the Father in Your Name would be given to them.*[109] I ask You today for the Church, that You might fill it with blessings and make it triumph over its enemies. I ask You for fervor for our communities, peace for all nations, purity and virtue for families and the reign of the Holy Spirit and of the Cross over all the world!

O my Mother, because of you I have the Eucharist, I have Jesus Who conquers me with His example and His tenderness! Holy Virgin, give me your heart to love Him, Who is Love. Amen.

Thoughts and Life

Not to lose time is one of the most difficult virtues to obtain. *To know how to be busy* is the science most useful for joy and virtue.

Commitment

Jesus, You chose me to bear fruit that will last. That is what You said to Your apostles, and I, in the measure of my strength, will communicate Your teachings to others.

+ Lord, I offer You many acts of gratitude for all the benefits granted to priests and religious.

+ Lord, please give families faith and generosity to be able to respond to Your call to their children.

---

[109] Cf. Jn 14:13.

I Am ⟨...⟩ Vine
and My Fat⟨...⟩ Vine Grower

⟨...⟩, the Vine that gives true Life,
⟨...⟩s to the weak to feed them
⟨...⟩His Blood and communicate
⟨...⟩Divine strength for sacrifice.

"I am the true Vin⟨...⟩ather is the Vine Grower" of the fruitful Vine that bears ⟨...⟩s of eternal life from which the true wine that begets v⟨...⟩xtracted, My Blood shed at the place of My sorrowful Passion.

My Father is the Vine Grower, Who cultivated this Vine Who is Your Jesus. He loves Me and sacrifices Me on your behalf. He loves Me with the infinite love of which only God is capable and nevertheless *gives His only Son for the salvation of the world.*[110] He, as a true farmer, planted, cultivated and cared for this plant with paternal tenderness, this Vine loaded with clusters of the most perfect virtues, born from the womb of Mary and watered continuously with heavenly graces.

My Father wants the branches united to Me, the Vine, to bear fruit; *"those who do not abide in Me will be thrown out like branches and wither."* They will bear no fruit and will dry out.

---

[110] Cf. Jn 3:17.

"But if you abide in Me and My words remain in you, you may ask whatever you wish and it will be done for you. In this is My Father glorified, that you bear much fruit and become My disciples."[111]

Remain in My love. Do you know what it means *to remain in My love?* It means to bring heaven close; not to follow your own desires but those of Jesus; even more, it means *to have with Him* the same love, feeling and being. It means to suffer, not looking at the earth but at the Cross, loving with patience, constancy and enjoyment. It means to follow a life of *prayer, self-denial and purity* without leaving Me, without being dissipated by the things of this world, without being troubled by adversity of any kind. It means always to be willing to fight again after each misfortune: it means to love, to love and to know that love makes everything that is difficult easy and everything that is bitter, sweet.

Stop living for yourself and give Me not only the flowers and the fruits but also the trunk, the branches and the roots. I want all the shoots for Myself, as all the Vine is for you.

Imitating Me, leave yourself in the hands of My Father, the Vine Grower, so that He thinks in your soul, lives in your body, loves in your heart; so that, *remaining in My love*, all your actions may have supernatural value and be a reproduction of the Vine itself.

If you do this your sacrifices and prayers will be efficacious, because, if you are united to Me, the Father will grant you whatever you ask.

Come to your Vine, Jesus, Who wants to nourish you with His substance. Come so that I introduce you to My Father, the Vine Grower, and tell Him that you are Mine, that My juice gives you life and that you only want to grow and develop in His hands. Come to be planted in the fruitful soil of My Eucharist.

---

[111] Jn 15:6-8.

Act of Thanksgiving

Jesus, I want to remain in Your love, being sanctified under the blessed hand of Your beloved Father, Who is also mine.

Sanctity is nothing other than the reproduction of Your life in us.

To be a saint is to do everything *for You*, for *Your love, because You are Who you are. With You* means *in union with You*, without ever losing sight of You and *in You* with great intimacy and holy confidence. It is to see with Your eyes, to hear with Your ears, to work with Your hands, to walk with Your feet, to feel with Your own Heart. Is it not true, Jesus, that this is what it means to remain in Your love? What horizons open before me with these words!

Here is Your little plant, wishing to be cultivated by the heavenly Father. I want to produce the fruits of virtue, *remaining in Your love*. I want all my faculties, all the energies of my will to be at the service of this supreme end — love! May this love unite me to You and make me remain always in You, abandoned to Your will.

Holy Mother, who as no other creature *remained* intimately united to your Jesus, obtain for me the grace to remove everything that separates me from Him! Amen.

Thoughts and Life

The trial of suffering makes us abide in love.

The glory of the Father is that we bear much fruit.

Commitment

At each tolling of the hour, I will try *to remain in Your love*, Jesus, since I do not know the time when You will call me.

+ Father, I ask You for the union with Jesus of all the universe and the Church.

+ May families live united to You, the true Vine.

23

I Am the Gate,
Whoever Enters Through Me Will Be Saved
(Jn 10:9)

> Jesus is the Gate through which one
> enters Paradise. It opens for
> whomever has lost the way and
> wants to find it. It invites him with
> love to do him good and to teach
> him how to be happy eternally.

"I am the Gate, whoever enters through Me will be saved; he will go in and out and find pasture."[112] Not only am I the Way, but also the Gate through which I want you to enter without hesitation, because whoever does not pass through Me cannot come to the Father nor enter the kingdom of heaven.

"Ask and you shall receive," I said one day. "Knock and it will be opened."[113] So that you would not pass through many gates that were not Me and in order that you would not be worn out by many roads, I had My Heart opened by a lance, so that you could enter through its gaping wound and have no trouble touching and entering into the innermost part of My Heart where all My treasures are stored.

I am Jesus, Who makes everything easy for your good. But swapping places, I find your heart closed and I am *"at the door knocking."*[114] I am the One Who loves you, and I am in the Eu-

---

[112] Jn 10:9.
[113] Cf. Mt 7:7; Lk 11:9.
[114] Rv 3:20.

charist asking you to open wide the door of your heart. I am the One Who is always seeking you, like a beggar, never tiring, waiting at the door of your heart.

Open, so that I may enter and enrich you with My graces. God did not want to be happy without men and for that reason the divine Word came down to the world, became Flesh in a Virgin and made Himself Eucharist.

So here I am. Take away all your obstacles, cleanse yourself with contrition, empty yourself of all sin, adorn yourself with *purity, humility and love.* I desire this in order to establish My dwelling in you.

"The Teacher is here asking for you."[115] I want to enter into you so that you, whom I love with a love of infinite predilection, might enter into Me. May your heart be not troubled for I am the God of peace, Who delights in making you happy.

Enter into Me. I want to show you your name written in My Heart and I want you to show Me Mine in yours, as I take possession of that which belongs to Me by right. Give Me all that you are: soul, life, senses, powers, affections and even your sins that I might forgive them.

What is stopping you? Come, you who are so far away. I open My Heart; open yours. Let us embrace each other with love, losing yourself in My Heart and I in yours. Come.

Act of Thanksgiving

Jesus, let us both enter by the doors of our hearts. I wish to enter through Yours and be saved. Enter into me and take possession of me.

Jesus, You, like a beggar, knock at the door of my heart and wait night and day to be heard. You, my Good, my sure

---

[115] Jn 11:28.

Hope, my *Gate to heaven*, reign in me, embrace me and make me catch fire in Your holy flames.

Jesus, I want to enter into Your Heart. You do not need to knock at my door, since it will be always open for You and closed to sin.

I am unworthy and a sinner, but Your pleasure *is to give*, Jesus. I stretch out my arms to You, Who will *never spurn a contrite and humble heart.*[116]

I give You my will, works and desires, body and soul, all that I am, have and could possess. Accept me, receive me and never leave what belongs to You.

Mary, mother of God and my Mother, close with a lock of love the doors of my being so that Jesus can never leave. Amen.

Thoughts and Life

To suffer, work and smile enjoying any cross.

To ask nothing, nor refuse anything.

I will not ask anything for me, but the pleasure of ceaselessly delighting my God.

Commitment

Jesus, I want to transform all my life into an offering for the greater glory of the Father. Your desires will be my desires, Your oblation, mine.

+ Lord Jesus, I offer today many acts of self-control in favor of those who assist the Pope.

+ May families enter through You, Jesus-Gate, Who leads us to the Father.

---

[116] Cf. Ps 50:19.

24

When You Lift Up the Son of Man You Will Come to Realize that I Am
(Jn 8:28)

> The victorious Christ, raised on the Cross, came to the world to attract everyone to Himself in order to teach us true love and to inflame us with strength and fortitude in the practice of virtues.

"When you lift up the Son of man you will come to realize that I am."[117]

Is it not true that nailed to the Cross is where you have known Me best?

Is it not true that looking at Me there, you have not been able to doubt My love?

Is it not true that a crucifix is a consolation in your life and that a glance towards it gives you fortitude, confidence, contrition and purity?

I knew all that, and in order that you would come to know Me, I embraced humiliations, suffering and martyrdom so that the voice of My Blood would resound in you and bring you to understand My love.

---

[117] Jn 8:28.

With the weapon of the Cross, I conquered the world. This is the only thing that secures the triumph and the victory. Love this holy weapon, kiss it with gratitude, for it is the seal of My chosen ones. By it I will know them as Mine on the last day. The Cross is a treasure by which you will merit heaven.

Do not be surprised that virtue costs. Think only that *"My yoke is easy and My burden light."*[118] Be not afraid. If you want to know Me and follow Me, *"take up your cross,"*[119] because sacrifice is the life of the saints and I want you to be one.

What is this? Does the road to Calvary make you tremble? *I am with you in the midst of tribulations* and united to Me, nothing is hard; rather, all is easy and agreeable.

Conquer yourself; I shall be your fortitude. Remember that only the one who struggles obtains the reward, because there is no victory without a battle, nor virtue without sacrifice. *The kingdom of heaven suffers violence,*[120] and the measure of your love will be that of your sacrifices, because only those and not words are proofs of love.

As an example, look at Me lifted high on Calvary and learn the extent of My affection. I never refused any suffering and with all generosity I gave My Blood and Life for you. If I let Myself be nailed to a hard piece of wood, I did so thinking of you, so that, seeing Me perpetuate My life on the altar, you would not doubt that *I am.*

"My son, give Me your heart,"[121] because I have conquered it with My suffering. Will you deny it? No, because you love Me, I know.

No one is worthy of Me, but love will shorten the distance.

---

[118] Mt 11:30.
[119] Cf. Mk 8:34; Lk 9:23.
[120] Mt 11:12.
[121] Pr 23:26.

Act of Thanksgiving

Jesus, You Yourself promised that *when You would be lifted up on the Cross You would attract all men to You.*[122]

So that I would know You, You crucify Yourself. In order to pardon me, You open Your Heart and with Your Blood and water You cleanse and purify me.

How can I not know You on that Cross, my Jesus, since You are the only One Who has loved me so? All my being is moved to see You dead for me, and more from the power of love than from suffering.

Jesus, my Redeemer, I adore You. I promise You to climb any calvary in order that You be with me. Live in me and take possession of my powers, affections, feelings, senses, blood and all that I am, so that You can exclaim: *You love Me and I will love you and My Father will love you and We will come to make Our dwelling in you.*[123]

Mary, at the foot of the Cross, you were crucified with your Divine Son, obtain for me the grace never to descend from the height of my crosses, that in them I may recognize your Jesus. Amen.

Thoughts and Life

If Jesus crucifies us with Him, it is to transform us in Him out of love.

In spite of the intensity of His sufferings on the Cross, Jesus only manifested sweetness, kindness, resignation and serenity.

We will practice these virtues until death because *it is in constancy that they are heroic.*

---

[122] Cf. Jn 12:32.
[123] Cf. Jn 14:23.

Commitment

To embrace the cross of each day, I will keep in my mind the Will of my beloved Father, Whom I wish to please in union with Jesus.

+ Lord, today I will offer many acts of mortification, in order to extend the kingdom of the Cross and so that all will know You and love the Church.

+ Jesus crucified, attract families to You, so that they will be sparks of love in the world.

25

I Am He

(Jn 18:5-8)

> Jesus, Who goes out to meet those
> who are going to arrest Him, comes
> to the coward who always runs
> away from suffering and any cross
> to teach him the strength of virtue
> and the love that fears nothing.

"I Am He," I answered the crowd of soldiers who on the night of My passion went out to arrest Me, making them fall to the ground. *"Who is it you want?"* I said after I had raised them up and they answered, *"Jesus, the Nazorean." "I have already told you that I am He. Now if I am the one you want, let these men go."*[124] Take Me, but do not touch those who are Mine, My disciples. Such is My loving Heart.

I am this same Jesus, only in diametrically opposed circumstances, because I know that you are looking for Me, not as a killer but as a loving child of the Eucharist. You look for Me as the Master of your life, to make reparation for the forgetfulness of the ungrateful and to console My Heart wounded by so many crimes.

Come to Me, since I am He Who comes to ask for your love and tenderness, your affections and tears, your senses, thoughts, and sufferings, and a pure heart on which to recline

---

[124] Jn 18:7-8.

My head. *I am He* Who loves you to the point of coming to be your daily nourishment, communicating to you My own substance.

I am *He Who loves you and gave Myself up for you.*[125] This is because true love does not count the calvaries, puts no conditions and throws itself with holy enthusiasm into performing sacrifices for the Beloved. I am He Who died nailed to a Cross to redeem you for heaven, to expiate your crimes, making Myself a slave, bread, *"a worm and not a man."*[126]

I am the Word Who made Myself Flesh to prove to you My love, to move you in your innermost being, to hear from your lips, *"I love You!"* My infinite love for you went to the point of this insanity!

Come, show Me your gratitude, tell Me about your aspirations, your desires, your hopes, your sorrows and all that afflicts you so that I can console you. *"Come to Me all of you."*[127]

Act of Thanksgiving

Jesus, You gave Yourself up to killers to be torn apart for me and how have I repaid You for your Blood and Life?

Lord, do not hide Your face from me.[128]

I love You and like St. Peter I will say, *"Leave me, Lord, for I am a sinful man."*[129] But, what would I do without You, my God, Who are always ready to forgive and do good to me, up to suffering for me?

---

125 Cf. Gal 2:20.
126 Ps 21:7.
127 Mt 11:28.
128 Ps 142:7.
129 Lk 5:8.

I want to live close to Your Eucharistic Heart.

Queen of Heaven, Sorrowful Mother, you who witnessed the humiliations, affronts and death of your Jesus, whisper in His ear how much I love Him.

Thoughts and Life

In virtue and love one never reaches an end. To the extent that one grows in love for God and neighbor, self-surrender and sacrifice increase.

Commitment

Holy Spirit, I will be docile to You Who teaches me to love Jesus to the utmost.

+ Lord, I will offer You today many acts of mortification for our Holy Father, the Pope and for Cardinals.

+ Holy Spirit, see to it that in homes true love shown in sacrifice reigns.

26

Are You the Christ, the Son of God?
It is You Who Said So
(Mt 26:64)

> Jesus, the Son of God made man
> out of love, comes to those He has
> chosen to tell them once more
> "I am your Jesus Who loves you
> so much."

That memorable night of My Passion, being at his house, Caiaphas said to Me: *"I order You in the name of the living God to tell us if You are the Christ, the Son of God."* *"You have said so,"* I replied. *"Moreover, I declare to you that from now on you will see the Son of man, seated at the right hand of Power, and coming on the clouds of heaven."*[130]

I told the truth for which I was judged and condemned to death. I was hit, slapped on the face without compassion, but I wanted to teach you never to lie so that if you would see yourself despised, without honor and even condemned to capital punishment for telling the truth, as My enemies did to Me, you would not mind! Always tell the truth. Do not let any human respect stop you. *"Whoever is ashamed of Me before men I will be ashamed of them before My heavenly Father."*[131]

---

[130] Mt 26:63-64.
[131] Mt 10:33.
[132] Cf. Heb 1:3.

"He Who is the splendor of the Father,"[132] was slapped, despised and made the scorn of men, without beauty. All for your love, to be your teacher in virtues, to show you the way to heaven that you want to follow.

What do you say? Is not your heart moved before a God, in Whose face you can see the fullness of beatitude, spat upon and bloody to give you a lesson never to forget? Put your hand over your heart and think about how you have betrayed truth and lacked the courage to confess My Name. That you might not be like this any more, prefer to die a thousand deaths than lie and always glory in being My disciple.

Do not come to the Mystery of love without love, because love is paid with love, and *"whoever loves much will be forgiven much."*[133] If you accuse yourself, God will excuse you and will open His arms and pour over you the balm of forgiveness.

Thus, come to My altar contrite and humble. My Heart palpitates strongly to go to your side. Come, so that I may put My Heart next to yours.

Act of Thanksgiving

"You are the Christ, the Son of the living God,"[134] yes. And far from judging You *guilty of death,*[135] I tell You that You are the Life of my life, and with all the tenderness that I can muster, I want to console You and tell You that for as long as my heart beats, it will be entirely for You.

Look upon me with mercy, take me for ever as Your own. Hide Yourself within me, cleansing me of every stain that could offend You. May Your fire penetrate me and Your light illumi-

---

[133] Cf. Lk 7:47.
[134] Mt 16:16.
[135] Mt 26:66.

nate me. May Your Blood comfort me and may Your Heart and virtues be mine.

Mary, from whom the face of Jesus took its beauty, look at how they have put on Him my sins. Mother of mine, promise Him for me that I would rather die than deny or offend Him. Amen.

Thoughts and Life

Do not despise small weaknesses since from them larger ones can come.

Do not trust your own strength, holiness or wisdom. Stay away from the occasions of sin and you will avoid sin.

Commitment

Crucified Jesus, taking pride in being Your disciple, I will not be conquered by sins of human respect.

+ Lord Jesus, I offer You today many acts of mortification for those who deny and persecute You.

+ Jesus, grant families that are persecuted for Your Name, the strength to proclaim their faith.

27

Are You the King of the Jews?
You Say So
(Mt 27:11)

> Jesus, the King of heaven, of earth
> and of all that exists, comes to the
> ungrateful to pardon them and tell
> them how much He loves them.

"I am a King, as you say." I affirmed in truth to Pilate when he said: *"So, You are a King?"*

Yes, certainly I am the universal King, but I wanted My crown in the world to be one of thorns and I only accepted this title on earth at *a humiliating trial and nailed to a Cross!* Thus, My kingdom was made public, to teach you that a Christian should only reign from the height of his calvaries.

This title was the occasion of mockery and sarcasm on the part of My enemies. *"All hail, King of the Jews,"*[136] they said mocking the eternal Majesty — and being made the laughingstock of men out of love for you, with a piece of purple cloth and a reed for a scepter, they spat on Me and beat Me.

Pilate, upon passing the sentence of death, declared, *"Here is your King!"* *"Take Him away and crucify Him,"* I heard, and the ingratitude broke My Heart. Pilate insisted: *"Shall I crucify your*

---

[136] Mt 27:29.

King?" *"We have no King but Caesar." "His blood be on us and our children,"*[137] they answered.

This precious Blood today pours over you. Your King sheds it willingly to cleanse you and to quench your thirst.

At each Mass, at each moment, to the end of time, the Divine Victim will willingly bend down for only one, for you, if you were the only one alive, because My love is infinite and stronger than all the crimes of the world.

Thus your King knows how to love. He knows how to make sacrifices for His children. *"I do not call you slaves, but friends,"*[138] and *"I did not come to be served by others but to serve,"*[139] I said. I am Jesus, the Nazarene, King of peace and love. As a King I crowned Myself with thorns the day of My espousal with the Church, that is the joy of My Heart. My throne was the Cross and My law, the law of love!

Behold, it is I, the One you contemplate in the Eucharist. I am King and bear your likeness within Me; I long to give Myself to you. Come close, then, to your heavenly crucified King. Open your heart because He wants to raise you up, to enrich you and divinize you. Come to be taught humility, simplicity and love.

Act of Thanksgiving

Merciful King, Who gives Yourself totally to all and totally to each one with Your celestial wealth in the Eucharist, I love You with all my heart and want to burn with the fire of a thousand volcanoes in Your honor.

---

[137] Jn 19:14-15; Mt 27:25.
[138] Jn 15:15.
[139] Mt 20:28.

"The kingdom of God is already in your midst,"[140] You said one day and today not only do I feel this kingdom inside of me, but the King Who rules with love.

Mother and Queen, I want to recognize Jesus, just as the good thief, repentant and humiliated, recognized Him as King. He saw Him dying and asked Him for life. He saw Him crucified and asked Him to take him to his kingdom. His eyes only saw crosses, but his faith saw the triumph. He saw Him die yet did not hesitate to put his whole confidence in Jesus-King.

Thoughts and Life

The Cross is the battleground of Divine love and the greatest victory is to conquer oneself.

"Never am I better than when I am not well," said St. Francis de Sales.

Commitment

Father, like Jesus, my happiness on earth is to love You and sacrifice myself for You.

+ Jesus, I will give You the gift of many acts of self-control for kings, rulers of the earth and the Holy Father, our Pope.

+ Jesus, may families proclaim with their lives that You are King and Lord.

---

[140] Lk 17:21.

28

Peace Be With You, It Is I

(Lk 24:36, 39)

Jesus, the King of Peace, He
Who conquered heaven with His
precious Blood, comes to the weak
in faith to console them, lifting
their hearts and filling them with
the riches of the peace of the
Holy Spirit.

My disciples were talking about Me, following My Resurrection, when suddenly, appearing in their midst, I said: *"It is I. Do not be afraid. Peace be with you."*[141]

I am the same Jesus Who is speaking to you now in the Eucharist, and I come to bring peace to your heart. Look at Me with faith and discover that *I am the Savior,* coming to bring you peace, the peace of the children of God, a peace that is not of this world but comes from conquering one's passions. This is because My peace is the victory obtained by charity on the Cross.

True peace is the tranquility of a heart that is self-possessed, without being disturbed or agitated.

Peace is the sweet freedom of spirit that does everything without anxiety.

---

141 Lk 24:36-38.

Peace is moderate and tranquil serenity without lethargy, ready to act without agitation.

This peace is the fruit of the Holy Spirit that I communicate to those who love Me. It is a priceless treasure, a gift of God, a celestial dew poured into pure hearts. I am the God of Peace. Open yourself and be not afraid.

You have come to know Me many times *"in the breaking of the bread,"*[142] as did My disciples at Emmaus. You have rejoiced in talking about Me, remembering Me in your conversations. I know how to reward the smallest act of love. I give you My Peace and I am ready to bring it to the bottom of your heart.

Remember that if there is purity of heart, there is peace; that without charity towards your neighbor, peace cannot exist; and that without mortification, it is transient and false. Practice, then, these virtues, establish them in you and peace will be with you and you will find happiness and fulfillment in spiritual joy.

Act of Thanksgiving

God of Peace, Who performs so many wonders in the heart that loves You. Who are You and who am I? Transform this earth worm, my Lord, with the fire that inflames me on contemplating You.

Jesus, Your charity led You to die for me amidst frightful torments and now You come after being resurrected to bring me peace, to infuse confidence, saying to me, *"Be not afraid."* You think of my needs and come to take care of them. You love me, good Jesus, to insanity! You pay no attention to the extremes of my ingratitude, but rejoice in manifesting Your mercy and goodness.

---

[142] Lk 24:35.

Give me, Lord, contrition for my sins, abnegation in sacrifice and a pure, humble and patient heart towards all those around me. With these virtues, I will have peace and with it I will have You, from Whom I never want to be separated.

Mary, you who are the Queen of Peace, teach me to love Him with your same ardor and tell Him that the measure of my love will be to love Him without measure. Amen.

Thoughts and Life

Faith is love that believes.
Hope is love that waits.
Adoration is love that prostrates itself.
Prayer is love that asks.
Mercy is love that forgives.
Charity is love that sacrifices itself.
Mortification is love that immolates itself.
Let us put this into practice and we shall have peace.

With St. Augustine, I will ask: "Why do I not have an infinite love to love the infinite Love?"

Commitment

Heart of Jesus, give me peace, so that my constant occupation is to love, losing myself in You.

+ Lord, I offer You today many acts of generosity that governments might always look for the good of their citizens.

+ Lord Jesus, may all homes enjoy Your peace.

29

Look at My Hands and My Feet;
It Is Really I
(Lk 24:39)

> Jesus shows His blessed wounds to
> those who do not believe unless
> they see and touch them. He comes
> to tell them that they can only know
> Him through love and suffering.

"Look at My hands and My feet; it is really I," I said to My
disciples in one of My apparitions after the Resurrection. This
is because, startled and frightened, they thought I was a ghost.
And because they were in a kind of daze, refusing to believe
their eyes, I went ahead and asked them for something to eat.

If you want to know Me, look at My hands and My feet,
that is to say, at *My wounds* which will reveal to you that *I am.*
These, *the marks of suffering*, bear witness to My love, the un-
equivocal sign by which you can know that I am your Jesus.
Look at My hands and My feet pierced more by your ingratitudes than by iron nails.

How many steps these feet took to find you and how many
blessings have you received from My hands, that have only been
busy pouring out benefits upon you? Not with a blazing fire,[143]
but with gifts of peace and love, I wanted to win your heart, to

---

[143] Cf. Heb 12:18-23.

give it life, *not by killing, but by dying, not by spilling your blood but Mine* on the Cross and on the altars. The fire that consumes My Heart now is not one of vengeance, but of infinite charity. And I want to pardon you more than you want to sin. *"Come close to Jesus the mediator of the new covenant that purifies you with His Blood."*[144]

I asked My disciples for something to eat, but to you I give My own Body and Blood in the Eucharist. Is this not love? What do you give Me for this excess of kindness? *"My Flesh is real food."*[145]

You already know Me. You have contemplated My hands and My feet. Do you not feel, do you not see that I am He Who invites you to calm the infinite desires of your heart? I loved you and gave Myself up to all sorts of sufferings and torments for you. Look at Me then, triumphant and victorious over death. I come also to you, so that by studying Me, you will know Who I am, and in knowing Me you will love your Jesus.

"It is My Father Who gives you the true Bread from heaven,"[146] the eucharistic Bread prepared for the salvation of all until the end of time.

Come close with humility, with unlimited confidence. Come so that I can make you happy.

Act of Thanksgiving

My good Jesus with Your pierced hands in mine, I contemplate with astonishment the tenderness of Your Heart. I want to study You, Jesus in Your infinite love for me. It is You.

---

[144] Heb 12:24.
[145] Jn 6:55.
[146] Jn 6:32.

I rejoice on seeing You so close to me, on perceiving Your purity and Your virtues. You want to give me Your Body, Your Blood and Your Heart with all its beats. You wish to die a thousand times on the altars to give me life and nothing seems too small for Your love in order to win me over.

How can I repay You for all Your infinite benefits? *I will deny my very self and lovingly take up my cross to follow You.*[147] With Your grace I will not fear, Lord, since You have shown me *"Your love to the end."*[148] When will my merits ever be exhausted, *since they are Yours?* My beloved Jesus, receive me at this hour with all that I am and have. Take me because I am Yours forever.

Mother of Him Who is my love, crucified and wounded in your heart with the wounds of your Divine Son, tell Him that He is my life, that I love Him and want to make my dwelling in His Heart of fire. Amen.

Thoughts and Life

I saw my Savior pierced by nails. I contemplated Him with love and found that *He was* mortification, *He was* suffering and *He was* love. Then a transformation was wrought in me and everything seemed to me Divine.

What does all suffering matter in order to have Jesus? Let us look for Him with ardor, but there where He wants to be found, up there on the Cross.

---

[147] Cf. Mt 16:24; Mk 8:34; Lk 9:23.
[148] Cf. Jn 13:1.

Commitment

To love You, Jesus, is to imitate You! And to imitate You, is to love and suffer.

+ Lord, I offer You today many acts of sacrifice for the propagation of the Apostleship of the Cross.

+ Jesus, You Who have loved us to the end, make families all over the world experience Your love and respond to it.

30

I Am Jesus, the One You are Persecuting
(Acts 9:5)

> Jesus persecuted wants to forgive.
> He comes to those who have sinned
> and have repented of their faults to
> teach them to love and to accept
> salvation.

"I am Jesus Whom you are persecuting,"[149] I answered St. Paul when he was blinded by the splendor of heaven on the way to Damascus and fell on the ground. Surprised on hearing his name, he had asked: *"Who are You, Lord?"* The moment that he heard Who I was, he replied: *"What do You want me to do?"* What a beautiful example of immediate response he gives you today!

I have also surrounded you with the splendor of heaven, in having you contemplate My doctrine. Many times have you also fallen at My feet, contrite and humble on seeing your sins and ingratitudes. You have heard in your innermost being My voice saying: See, you persecute Me by being proud, sensual, envious, gossipy, avaricious, lazy, angry, etc.

These attitudes hurt your neighbor, harm you and wound My Heart, Whose essence is charity.

Why do you persecute Me in your brethren? Why do you

---

[149] Acts 9:5.

persecute Me, rejecting the commandment to love? What have I done to you but provide you with benefits? Why do you despise Me and why, in front of men, are you ashamed to belong to Me? Why the ambition, hatred, vengeance, indifference and many other things, *that only you and I know*, that offend My Heart Whose only crime is to love you?

Why do you crown Me with thorns through your lukewarmness? Why do you deny Me through your sins of human respect? Why do you prefer temptations to My grace? Why do you seek yourself, soil your very being with vainglory and crucify Me with your bad example? Why do you persecute Me? Why?

What could I have done for you that I have not done? Have I not given you your being, food, joy, health, natural gifts, gifts of grace: glory, Redemption, the Sacraments, My Blood and My Body in the Eucharist, to take away your sins? Why so much ingratitudes for this loving Heart that allowed itself to be pierced for you?

My life, My merits and My death were for you and My glory, My eternal rewards will be for you. Is it not true that you will not persecute Me from now on?

I hope so, little one, whom I cover with My pardon and mercy. One act of sincere repentance, no matter how small, is enough to make Me forget one hundred years of persecution and horrendous crimes. I am the God of Love and I am more ready to forgive you, than a mother is to free her child from a fire. Be not afraid and come to Me with full confidence. If I have numbered your crimes, I did so to cover them then with My mercy and wash them with My Blood.

Come then, little lost lamb. I am your Father. I am your Shepherd, I am your Jesus Whom you have persecuted, but Whom you will love from now on with all your strength. Come repentant to Me.

Act of Thanksgiving

Jesus, open my eyes as You did those of Saul and give me a guide to direct my life. Teach me the law of love. From the depths of my misery I say to You, full of confidence, *"Lord, what would You have me do?"*

Good teacher, teach me Your ways. *"A clean heart create for me, O God, and a steadfast spirit renew within me, to bring me to You."*[150]

I put myself in Your hands, as a poor instrument, full of enthusiasm and zeal to extend Your Name, to let the world know You, to proclaim You to all hearts, to give my blood and my life for You.

No matter how much I might sin, infinitely greater would Your forgiveness be. I want to glorify You, even though I have to suffer, so that like St. Paul You would show me *how much I have to suffer for Your Name.*[151] What do I gain if I wish to repair my faults, if I want to proclaim the Cross with my example?

"The world has been crucified to me and I to the world." "Far be it for me to boast of anything but the Cross of our Lord Jesus Christ."[152] I want to experience a superabundance of joy in the midst of sorrows, persecutions and torment of any kind, for I know that I can do all things in Him who comforts me.[153]

"What can separate me from the love of Christ?" I will repeat with Your apostle, *"neither hunger nor thirst nor the sword, neither death nor life will be able to separate me from You."*[154] Give me Your love since *"love is everything, and if I had all the virtues and could move mountains, but did not have love, I would be nothing."*[155]

---

[150] Ps 50:12.
[151] Cf. Acts 9:16.
[152] Gal 6:14.
[153] Cf. Ph 4:12-13.
[154] Rm 8:35.
[155] Cf. 1 Cor 13:2.

Jesus, give me the fire that inflamed St. Paul, so that I may love You and make You loved unto giving my blood and life for You.

Mary, Refuge of sinners, precious vessel of election, as St. Paul was, my Mother, give me this love more powerful than death to consume me by living only for Jesus, to be able to say in truth: *"To live is Christ."*[156] *"It is no longer I who live, but Christ Who lives in me."*[157]

Thoughts and Life

To be nothing, to be a lot, to be little; to command, to obey; to be humiliated, forgotten; to face needs or to have an abundance; to enjoy or be overwhelmed with work; to be alone or in company; to discover a long road ahead of me or not be able to see more than the exact space to put my foot; to be consoled or suffer dryness; to be sick or healthy; to be a burden or a help; to live long or to die early. All will be equally accepted by me in conformity with the will of God.

Commitment

Father, I will be from now on a living *Yes* to Your dispositions, an *Amen* to Your Will. I will accept everything to expiate for my sins, being ready for Your loving communication.

+ Lord, *what do You want me to do* in favor of our Holy Father, cardinals, archbishops, bishops, diocesan priests, missionaries and consecrated laity?

+ Lord Jesus, may each one of the members of our families have a living encounter with You.

---

[156] Ph 1:21.
[157] Gal 2:20.

31

And You, Who Do You Say That I Am?
(Mt 16:15)

> Jesus looks for His creatures,
> comes to those who are moved by
> His infinite tenderness, and takes
> pleasure in hearing from their
> own lips Who He is.

"Who do men say that I am? And you, Who do you say that I am?" I asked My disciples in confidence one day, and Peter, answering for all, replied: *"You are the Christ, the Son of the living God."*[158]

Today, in this day of intimacy with Me, you hear My lips repeating in your ears this same question: *And you, Who do you say that I am?* Speak, I want to listen. I want to hear and know what you think of Me. Give Me your impressions.

One thing only is necessary for Me: *love, love and only love.* If you love Me, be not afraid, empty your heart into Mine. If you love Me, you would have known, studied and reproduced Me in your heart. You would have drunk and fed on the Eucharist.

Those who love Me would recognize Me in a thousand worlds, should they exist. These are the ones who, in wonder, exclaim in all of life's circumstances, *"It is the Lord,"*[159] and who

---

[158] Mt 16:16.
[159] Cf. Jn 21:7.

in every event, good or bad, turn to Me with eyes of faith and adore My ever benevolent will.

Tell me, what you know about Me, what you tell others, your desire to love Me, your zeal that others love Me, what you feel, think and believe, what you are unable to contemplate.

Who *do you say* that I am? Answer Me, for I have already seen your tears. Tell Me Who I have been for you, little earth worm, Who I am, Who I will be if you are faithful.

Answer Me: *Who do you say that I am?*

Act of Thanksgiving

Lord, Who do I say that You are? The God of my heart and my eternal inheritance, the Infinite, the Word made Flesh, the Savior of my life, Jesus my beloved, my joy, my hope and the only treasure of my heart.

You are, Lord, the warmth of my existence, the light of my eyes, the breath of my mouth, the fire of my heart, the palpitations of all my being. You are my realized ideal, the One I love with all the titles of tenderness that can exist such as father, mother, brother, spouse, friend, all mothers to their children, with the same fire a thousand times in each breath and heartbeat, in each moment multiplied ad infinitum.

Help me to express *that You are* the only One worthy of all loves, the sovereign, thrice holy, Who humbled Himself because He willed to do so. You are the Jesus of the manger, of the desert, of Nazareth, the Jordan, Tabor, the One of the miracles, at the Cenacle, the Garden, the scourging, the insults, the thorns, the Cross, the Resurrection, Emmaus, the Ascension, Jesus of the Eucharist. My God and my Lord, all abnegation and love!

You are all modesty, humility, purity, silence, martyrdom, obedience, *love* and in this last word all the rest is condensed.

I would like to say something and I say nothing, because Your agonies and triumphs, Your example and virtues can be felt but not explained.

Jesus, You are… but why babble about *what You are?* You Yourself with Your human lips have told us in Your holy Gospel *what You are.* Therefore, each time that I am asked, *"Who is He?"* I will give the same answer that I shall give to You. With Your own voice I will respond, using some of the beautiful titles in the Gospel.

Who do you say that I am? You are the Good Shepherd, the Vine, the Bread of Life, the Way, the Truth and the Life, the One Who speaks with me (the Samaritan woman). You are the Son of God, the Resurrection and the Life, the Beginning of all things, the Light of the World, the Door to Salvation, the King, Jesus Whom men persecute, Who has chosen us, the Teacher Who is in the Father and in Whom the Father is. You are from above and I from below, the Messiah, seated at the right hand of the majesty of God, Who will come on the clouds of heaven, the true Vine and Your Father is the Vine Grower. You Yourself have shown us Your pierced hands and feet. You are the One crucified on high Whom we have come to know as Savior. *You are Who You are.* Who can say more? If we do not believe *Who You are,* we will die in our sins.

Is it not true that You are all this? You are the One Who transforms me, cleanses and purifies me by contrition and fills me with love. You are He Who walks with me in my calvary, making the cross easy and desirable. Thank you, Jesus, I say full of holy fire.

Mary, you knew all the heartbeats, movements and desires of Jesus. You who had engraved in yourself His features and virtues, I ask you today to obtain for me a *purity of heart* that reflects Jesus so that I may see Him always. Obtain for me on earth the Divine promise: *"Blest are the pure of heart for they shall see God."*[160]

---

[160] Mt 5:8.

Thoughts and Life

"Come, you blessed of My Father. Receive the kingdom prepared for you from the foundation of the world. For I was hungry and you gave Me to eat, I was thirsty and you gave Me to drink, I was a stranger and you took Me in, naked and you clothed Me. I was sick and you cared for Me, in prison and you came to Me."[161] But when was this? *"Amen, I say to you, insofar as you did it for one of these least of My brothers, you did it for Me."*[162]

This is the practical way to show today our love for Jesus Himself. Alms do not deprive us and He blesses mercy more than sacrifice.

Commitment

Jesus, I will see Your Name written on the forehead of the poor and with Your love I will help them without hesitation. One can do what one wants to do.

What do you do to support such a numerous family?, I asked a mother. She answered smiling: *Love!* When one loves, nothing is counted.

Jesus is there in the poor. *It is He!* Let us lavish our tenderness on them. Jesus is in the Eucharist. *It is He! Let us adore Him,* and with a pure heart let us receive Him all the days of our life in Holy Communion.

+ Holy Spirit, inflame all priests and families with Your love.

+ Mary, in your mother's heart is the life of priests and families. Intercede for all of them.

Jesus, Savior of Men,
Save them!

---

[161] Mt 25:34-36.
[162] Mt 25:40.

The Eucharist is the memorial of the surrender that the Father made of His Divine Son to men. This is why the Eucharist — celebrated, received, adored and lived — is the most perfect act of love from men to God, as a response to this highest manifestation of Divine Love.

A perfect model of this transformation and following of the Lord, as well as of a total giving of oneself to others is the Virgin Mary. She was docile to the Word of God and teaches us to be obedient also to His Divine Son, Jesus, Who is "the Way, the Truth, and the Life" (Jn 14:6).*

---

* Words of the Holy Father on the 100th anniversary of the Sisters of the Cross, May 3, 1997, nn. 3,5. The religious of the Cross of the Sacred Heart of Jesus, a community of sisters of contemplative life, unite themselves to the eucharistic oblation of Jesus at the celebration and adoration of the Eucharist, day and night for the glory of the Father and the salvation of all men, especially priests. Thus they live their baptismal priesthood in the simple and hidden offering of their daily life in profound communion with the Church and the world.

CONCEPCIÓN CABRERA DE ARMIDA

Mexican woman, wife, mother, and lay apostle

500,000 of her books were distributed anonymously in Europe and America during her lifetime and continue to this day setting hearts on fire with the love of Jesus and an ardent desire to collaborate in the salvation of all men and women in the world.

An Apostle of the Eucharist. Her first book *Before the Altar* was written to promote love of the Eucharist and has had more than 40 editions in four languages. She wrote these eucharistic meditations taken from the Gospel in 1912. 16,000 were rapidly distributed in Spain and throughout Latin America.

The present publication was issued to commemorate the Eucharist in the Jubilee Year: the 2000th anniversary of the Incarnation of the Word.

The Servant of God, Concepción Cabrera de Armida (Conchita) was born in San Luis Potosí, the 8th of December, 1862 and died in Mexico, D.F. the 3rd of March, 1937. The cause of her beatification is well underway.

FÉLIX DE JÉSUS ROUGIER *
French priest

Discovered in
Concepción Cabrera de Armida
a Mexican lay person

a deep experience of God and the gift to communicate this experience, able to provoke a living encounter with God in the person who gets in touch with her writing.

Father Félix, aware that this gift is for the universal Church, prepared its way in Europe. He had her books translated into English, French and German to enliven the faith through this grace that the Lord gives to the People of God.

The Holy Spirit loves diversity and achieves the wonders of a fruitful communion for the good of many.

Man - woman
Priest - lay person
European - American

---

* (1859-1938) Founder of the Missionaries of the Holy Spirit and three Congregations of women: Daughters of the Holy Spirit, Guadalupan Missionaries of the Holy Spirit, Oblates of Jesus-Priest.

He gave impulse to the Works of the Cross. He promoted the integral growth of thousands of lay persons and communicated to them something of his own apostolic zeal so that they might spread the love of the Holy Spirit and transform the world through his Action.